KETO
Breads™

35 Chewy & Delicious, Keto-Friendly Breads with 5 g NET Carbs or Less

Kelley Herring

By Kelley Herring & The Editors of Healing Gourmet®
©2017-2018. Copyright Health-e Enterprises.

Recipes

ROLLS & BUNS

CRACKERS, CROUTONS & CRUSTS

HEALTHY SUBSTITUTIONS

A Personal Note
FROM THE AUTHOR OF KETO BREADS

There are few foods more comforting and enjoyable than bread…

Whether it is a warm piece of focaccia dipped in olive oil… a chewy baguette… flaky croissant… a sandwich piled with your favorite meats… crusty pizza with bubbly, melted cheese… or even the simplest slice of toast, topped with butter…

The taste of bread takes us to culinary heaven. Even the smell is intoxicating. And the blissful "intoxication" you experience is real. In fact, you might say bread is the original food addiction.

Compounds in wheat engage the same receptors in your brain triggered by drugs of addiction, like heroin. That would certainly explain the feeling of euphoria! And just to make sure you keep coming back for more, the blood sugar spike induced by high-carb bread elevates dopamine – often called "the craving neurochemical".

Our love affair with bread is as old as recorded history. The Bible practically commands followers to eat it: *"Give us this day our daily bread…"* And in ancient Greece, it was so revered that the rest of the meal was called *ópson* – meaning "condiment" or bread's accompaniment.

However, the warm-and-fuzzy glow you experience when indulging in traditional bread is short lived and, unfortunately…

THOSE FEW MOMENTS OF BLISS CARRY A HEAVY PRICE

Well-known cardiologist, Dr. William Davis, calls wheat "the perfect chronic poison." And for a poison, we sure eat lots of it. The average American consumes 55 pounds of wheat flour every year, making refined flour the number-one source of calories in the American Diet!

Nutritional and functional medicine expert, Chris Kresser, describes this as "a public health catastrophe." And it's one you have likely experienced firsthand...

Eating traditional bread can elicit a range of unhealthy (and uncomfortable) symptoms. It might make you feel sluggish and foggy headed. It can cause you to gain unsightly fat on your belly, butt and thighs – while packing on deadly visceral fat around your internal organs.

It can also cause painful and embarrassing digestive symptoms – and is one of the leading causes of leaky gut, inflammatory bowel disease and an array of autoimmune conditions.

And if that's not enough, the glycemic index of wheat is among the highest of all foods. According to research published in the *American Journal of Clinical Nutrition*, eating just two slices of whole wheat bread spikes your blood sugar more than drinking a can of soda, eating a candy bar or just helping yourself to six teaspoons of table sugar![1]

High blood sugar levels are correlated with every chronic disease, including cancer, heart disease, Alzheimer's, diabetes, macular degeneration, physical aging (wrinkles!) and more.

And unfortunately, the so-called "healthy alternatives" are not so healthy at all.

MOST "GLUTEN-FREE" BREAD IS WORSE FOR YOUR HEALTH THAN THE REAL THING!

Many gluten-free products in the store – and even many recipes online – are made with high-glycemic starches that can increase your blood sugar faster and higher than wheat itself!

No surprise why most people actually GAIN weight on a "gluten-free" diet. A study published in the *American Journal of Gastroenterology* showed that 81% of people who adopted a gluten-free diet weighed more at the end of two years![2]

And due to the use of brown rice flour and brown rice syrup, some of these products also contain high levels of arsenic. Analysis by *Consumer Reports* showed that some popular gluten-free products contain up to 90 times more arsenic than what is allowed in drinking water![3, 4]

> *"These powdered starches are among the few foods that increase blood sugar higher than even whole wheat. It means these foods trigger weight gain in the abdomen, increased blood sugars, insulin resistance, diabetes, cataracts, and arthritis. They are NOT healthy replacements for wheat."*
>
> Dr. William Davis
> Author, *Wheat Belly*

But it's not all bad news today... in fact, I have great news!

You don't have to give up your enjoyment of fresh-baked bread, right from the oven. You don't have to forego the pleasure of a hot stack of French toast... a cheeseburger on a real bun... or a crusty piece of garlic bread to go with your Bolognese and meatballs.

And you can say goodbye to the temptation to "cheat" on your low-carb, ketogenic, grain-free or Paleo diet... because you can still enjoy ALL your favorite rolls, biscuits, bagels, sandwiches, pizza and more!

YOU REALLY CAN HAVE YOUR BREAD... AND BE WELL TOO!™

You don't have to choose between your daily bread and being healthy. You just have to choose healthy bread. And that's exactly what you're about to enjoy.

The recipes in this book use **functional ingredients** that actually protect – not wreck – your health. These breads are **metabolic power foods** that can help you sculpt a lean physique, instead of puffing up your muffin top!

And best of all is how they taste. These are not second-rate imitations that pale in comparison to the real thing. Some of these breads will be among the best you've ever enjoyed – with the same texture, taste and aroma you know and love.

I'm talking about REAL bread that is truly healthy – and yet so authentically delicious you will never miss the grain and carb-filled bread you used to eat. If you're tired of unhealthy alternatives and weak imitations, it's time to put real bread back on the table – guilt free!

But first, it's important you understand how these recipes were created and why they are so special.

I HAD A VERY PERSONAL REASON TO SOLVE THIS DIETARY DILEMMA

When I was in college – in the midst of an intensive pre-medical curriculum – I became very sick. I had extreme fatigue... never-ending sinus infections... digestive distress... and a trail of sores leading down my esophagus that did not heal for months.

I wasn't sure if my illness would ever end... or if it would be the end of me.

After two years of suffering – and no help from more than a dozen doctors – I decided to follow a very strict "elimination" diet. I got rid of almost all the foods I was eating. It was no fun at all! But within days, my throat began to heal. I regained my energy. My digestion normalized.

And before long, I charted a course back to health.

I later learned that I had developed a leaky gut – probably the result of **inflammatory grains** in my diet. This led to multiple food allergies and intolerances (including gluten) and progressed to an autoimmune condition – hence the unrelenting sores in my throat.

I was thrilled for the misery to be over and to have my health and energy back.

Because of my experience, I also had a very personal interest in the biology and chemistry classes of my pre-medical program. And while I chose not to become a doctor, I soon dedicated my career to the study of **nutritional biochemistry**.

I began to dissect and categorize hundreds of scientific studies about how foods can impact our long-term health. I also founded a company, **Healing Gourmet**, to provide life-saving education on the power of foods and nutrients to promote health and protect against disease.

In the midst of my own life and death struggle, I discovered the true purpose of my life.

But I was also growing frustrated with the restrictions in my diet. I missed the simple pleasures of the comfort foods I used to enjoy. I wanted to enjoy those delicious foods again – without worrying about my health or my waistline!

I have always been passionate about the culinary arts. It is the kitchen, where my heart is truly at home, cooking, baking and creating recipes. And that is why...

I MADE IT MY MISSION TO CREATE HEALTHY VERSIONS OF CLASSIC COMFORT FOODS

More than a decade ago, I set out to discover how to use "**intelligent ingredients**" to achieve all the attributes you love about bread... *without* the gluten, grains and carbs.

My goal was to create real bread with good-for-you ingredients that truly support your health goals. No inflammatory grains. No high-carb starches. No blood sugar spikes. No digestive disturbances. And a taste so delicious it could be served in a fine restaurant.

It was a very tall order – to say the least!

At the time, most people had not even heard the term "gluten free." There were very few grain-free bread recipes online (and most produced unappetizing results). There were no guidebooks to follow and no products in the store to model.

What I thought might take a few months, took years, because...

I HAD TO LITERALLY REINVENT THE RULES OF BAKING

I'm sure you've heard a lot of bad things about gluten over the years. But gluten does have a "good" side. Many of the properties we love most about bread are because of gluten.

It helps create that crusty-on-the-outside, chewy-on-the-inside texture. It provides stability and structure and helps bread to rise. Gluten is what makes pizza dough crusty, chewy and stretchy.

Baking is the science of chemistry. And baking with grain-free, low-glycemic ingredients is an exact science. You cannot simply replace wheat flour with almond or coconut flour and expect a recipe to "magically" achieve the characteristics of bread.

Every recipe in this book is the result of testing dozens of variations – swapping ingredients, changing amounts, adjusting ratios, testing preparation methods, cooking times and temperature. You wouldn't believe the difference one small change can make!

Over the years – after hundreds of trial-and-error formulations – we finally "cracked the code" and learned the secrets to...

CREATE GOOD-FOR-YOU BREADS AS DELICIOUS AS THE CLASSIC ORIGINALS YOU KNOW AND LOVE

In 2014, **Healing Gourmet** published our recipes in a book called, **Better Breads**. We knew a "few" people wanted to enjoy healthy bread, but we had no idea the response it would generate.

Better Breads was an instant success, as more than 100,000 people from around the world discovered you really can have your bread... AND be well too.™

Over the years, we have received hundreds of letters from readers. Many of these people had not eaten bread – or anything like it – for years. The ingredients in traditional bread were simply too damaging to their health. We heard stories of people crying tears of joy that they could finally take a bite of a real sandwich again.

Others were simply grateful that they could enjoy their favorite comfort foods – without "falling off the wagon" and cheating on their healthy diet!

We were thankful for the praise, but we knew the recipes could be even better. And we knew they could be PERFECT for the ketogenic diet. So, we selected the best of the best and continued to improve them.

We made the preparation methods simpler, improved the mix of ingredients and added new and better recipes to the collection. We continued testing until each one was perfect – and perfectly keto friendly.

And, of course, we took beautiful pictures of our creations along the way!

Keto Breads is the result of this gradual, continual and relentless improvement. The recipes in this book represent more than 10 years of dedicated efforts in the **Healing Gourmet** test kitchen. I truly believe they are the best tasting – and healthiest – grain-free and low-carb bread recipes in the world today.

I sincerely hope you enjoy these classic breads as much as we have enjoyed creating them for you. We hope that baking these creations will bring you joy – and get you closer to the body and health you deserve!

Have Your Bread... AND Be Well Too!

Kelley Herring
Founder, Healing Gourmet

1. Jenkins DH, Wolever TM, Taylor RH, et al. Glycemic index of foods: a physiological basis for carbohydrate exchange. Am J Clin Nutr. 1981 Mar; 34(3):362–6.
2. Dickey W, Kearney N. Overweight in celiac disease: prevalence, clinical characteristics, and effect of a gluten-free diet. Am J Gastroenterol. 2006 Oct;101(10):2356-9.
3. https://www.consumerreports.org/cro/magazine/2012/11/arsenic-in-your-food/index.htm
4. https://www.consumerreports.org/content/dam/cro/magazine-articles/2012/November/Consumer%20Reports%20Arsenic%20in%20Food%20November%202012_1.pdf

The Keto Solution™

30-Day Fast-Track System for a Better Body & Sharper Brain

Discover How You Can Easily Follow a
100% Ketogenic Diet While Still Enjoying
<u>ALL the Foods You Love</u>
(And Spending 70% Less Time in the Kitchen)!

www.KETOSOLUTION.net

Before You Bake:
A FEW REMINDERS

It wasn't easy to develop these recipes. The breads in this book are the result of hundreds of trials over a period of years. But all of those efforts have made it very easy for you!

We worked hard to simplify the preparation of each recipe. Most can be made in just 15-20 minutes of hands-on time. And you don't need to be an experienced baker to achieve superior results.

If you can mix a few ingredients in a bowl, shape the dough into a ball or drop it in a pan, and then slide it into the oven... you can make these breads. It's that easy!

In this section, we cover the finer points about baking these recipes, with specific tips to help you achieve the best results. This information is important, so please read this before baking your first recipe.

MEASUREMENTS & CONVERSIONS

There is an art to baking bread. But it is primarily a science – the science of chemistry. And as with any chemical formula, the slightest variation can make a big difference in the end result. This is why we provide **gram weights** for most dry ingredients.

Most American recipes measure ingredients by volume: teaspoons, tablespoons and cups. But volume measurements can be inaccurate, especially when it comes to powdered ingredients.

For example, there can be a significant difference in the amount of coconut flour in a cup, depending on whether the material is densely packed or loosely scooped. You can nearly double the weight by packing it tightly.

To minimize potential variations, we provide the **exact to-the-gram measurements** we used to create these recipes. If you don't already have a kitchen scale that measures in grams, it is an inexpensive investment that may improve your results. Most are available for about $10.

You certainly don't *need* a scale to make these recipes. We also provide volume measurements for every ingredient. And this isn't really an issue with a "half teaspoon of salt." So don't get carried away measuring to the fraction of a gram. Just get as close as you can to the amount called for, whether you decide to measure or weigh.

You will also see **metric measurements** provided for temperatures and liquid volumes. This is so our many friends around the world don't have to go searching for conversions. We want to make it easy for you too!

STOCKING YOUR PANTRY & KITCHEN

When I first began creating grain-free bread recipes, many of the ingredients were not available in most stores. I had to go direct to the manufacturers or locate a health food store that carried what I needed.

Thankfully, due to the popularity of the Paleo and ketogenic diets – and growing understanding of the damage that inflammatory grains and high-glycemic flours can do to your health – the demand for these ingredients has skyrocketed. These are no longer "specialty items."

You should be able to find most of the ingredients you will need in any well-stocked grocery or health food store. If you cannot find something locally, they are all carried by multiple suppliers on Amazon at a reasonable cost.

In some cases, we mention a specific brand (all of which are available on Amazon). However, if you live outside the United States and can't find the exact brand, don't worry. Just focus on locating the actual **ingredient.**

Canadian readers might consider purchasing ingredients from Bulk Barn. And international readers might consider iHerb.com. This company carries thousands of food, supplement and personal care products – with discounted shipping options to over 150 different countries: https://www.iherb.com/info/globalshipping

A FEW IMPORTANT NOTES ABOUT INGREDIENT SPECIFICATIONS

If you or someone in your family has an **allergy** or **intolerance** to almonds, eggs, coconut or dairy, you will be glad to know there are simple substitutions for these ingredients. So, you can still enjoy the delicious recipes in this book, without the ingredients that might trigger a reaction. If you're interested, please see the section at the end of this introduction, titled, Allergies, Intolerances & Healthy Substitutions.

Most of the recipes in this book call for "almond flour." There are two important considerations when choosing **almond flour**. First, be sure the almonds have had the skins removed. This is known as **"blanched" almond flour** and will produce the best results.

You also want to be sure the almonds are finely milled to a flour-like texture. Some brands sell almond "meal", which is often more coarsely ground and may not produce optimal results. You might also find some almond flour described as "culinary grade." This just means it is milled extra fine and is sold at a higher price. It might help your breads to achieve a slightly more uniform texture, but is not necessary.

Please also note that all eggs used in our recipes are **large eggs**. When egg "whites" are called for, feel free to use organic **liquid egg whites** from a container if you prefer. These are widely available from most grocers. And if possible, seek out farm-fresh eggs from your local organic farmer to get the highest levels of nutrients and healthy fats. Pastured eggs are one of Mother Nature's superfoods!

You may notice that a few recipes call for small amounts of Paleo-friendly starches like **tapioca** and **arrowroot**. These ingredients provide lift and stretch to the recipes in which they appear. However, as starches, they do contain higher levels of carbohydrates than the low-carb flours we primarily rely upon.

The first thing to remember is that these ingredients are used sparingly – as little as half a teaspoon and up to a few tablespoons in the whole recipe. So, while these individual ingredients may be higher in carbs, each serving of these breads contains just three to five grams of carbohydrate.

To put that in perspective, most people can achieve and maintain nutritional ketosis by keeping carbohydrates under 50 grams per day. Even very strict adherents to keto allow 20 to 30 grams daily. In this context, these breads are still perfectly "keto friendly."

If you would like to reduce the carbohydrates in those recipes even further, you can substitute these starches on a 1:1 basis with **hi- maize resistant starch**, **oat fiber** (not oat flour) or **lupin flour** – all of which are available on Amazon.

However, while these substitutions will make the resulting bread lower in carbohydrates, the results may differ slightly from the photos in the book. In addition, these are not ingredients we recommend, due to the fact they are grain and legume based and undergo extensive chemical processing.

In every recipe we formulate, we consider the health benefits of the ingredients and the quality of the resulting recipe first and foremost. Just because something is ketogenic or low-carb does not necessarily make it healthy!

And finally, a few words about **organic psyllium husk powder**…

About half the recipes in this book include this ingredient. And while they call for only a small amount, it is very important. I might even describe psyllium as a critical "secret" ingredient.

If you've heard of psyllium husk before, it is probably for its ability to "cleanse" the digestive system and promote regularity. It has also been shown to reduce appetite and improve blood sugar balance. These are all nice benefits. But the reason we use psyllium is for its remarkable properties in baking.

The combination of psyllium and eggs creates a strong protein network in the dough. This traps gas and steam and is a big benefit when you want bread – particularly one without yeast or gluten – to rise.

The "mucilaginous" fiber in psyllium is also gluey and gelatinous. In other words, it shares a number of physical properties with gluten. Psyllium helps to provide the spongy structure and stretchy texture that you know and love about breads that contain gluten.

We should also point out that while psyllium provides gastrointestinal *benefits* to most people, a small number are more sensitive to its effects. For these people, **supplemental doses** can cause digestive discomfort.

However, please note that the amount of psyllium used in these recipes is very low – typically one tablespoon or less in an entire loaf of bread. So, while you may notice improved regularity, it will not be the same as taking a typical supplemental dose – unless you eat the whole loaf!

IMPORTANT: These recipes call for **psyllium husk POWDER** – not the whole husk. While the nutrition facts are the same, **whole husk** and

psyllium powder perform very differently in baking. Due to increased surface area, the powder absorbs more moisture and does so more rapidly.

So always use a product that is powdered (or blitz whole husk in a coffee grinder until it is a fine powder). Otherwise, your dough may turn out more like soup!

And because psyllium crops may be sprayed with pesticides, we recommend organic. The brand we use is made by *Starwest Botanicals*.

Now, let's address one of the most common questions we receive...

HOW TO GET THE BEST "RISE" FROM YOUR BREADS

The bottom line is that these breads are not going to rise to the same extent as traditional high-carbohydrate breads that contain gluten. In some cases, traditional breads can double in size during "proofing" and then continue to rise in the oven.

The yeast breads in this book will generally rise by 20 to 30 percent before baking and a bit more in the oven. They simply do not have the level of carbohydrates (and gluten) required to double in size. However, by following the recipes exactly, you can easily replicate the results pictured in this book.

And there are a few tips to ensure your breads rise to their fullest potential...

Most important is that you **choose the correct-sized loaf pan.**

If you use a pan larger than what is specified in the recipe, the dough or batter may spread out – instead of rising up. If you do not have a pan of the exact size specified, it is better to use one that is smaller, rather than larger.

There are three sizes of loaf pans called for in this book: 9" x 5" | 8" x 4" | 7.5" x 3.5"

The two larger pans are widely available. However, you may have trouble finding the smaller pan in the exact size above. If so, don't worry. Quite a number of companies make pans very close to this size that work just fine. We created a list of these pans and where they can be found on our resources page, which you can access here: https://ketobreads.net/resources/

Your best bet is to follow the recipes exactly. However, in case you need to improvise, the best "rule of thumb" for selecting the correct-sized loaf pan is that the dough or batter should come three-quarters up the side of the pan. This will help you achieve the perfect "domed" loaf.

If possible, choose baking pans made of steel. You may find that some available options are made of aluminum. That's fine too – but we do not recommend allowing your bread to come in contact with aluminum. It can leach and is associated with serious health concerns.

The best way to mitigate the concern is to use a "sling" made of unbleached parchment paper. Grease the pan with butter, avocado or coconut oil, so there is something for the parchment to stick to. Then cut a piece of parchment large enough to cover the bottom and sides of the pan. This also helps keep the bread from sticking.

The next tip for getting the best rise from your **Quick Breads** – breads made *without* yeast – is to bake immediately after mixing the ingredients.

Quick Breads rise as the result of a chemical leavening process, where a weak acid (usually apple cider vinegar or lemon juice) is combined with a weak base (usually baking soda or baking powder). The combination produces carbon dioxide gas. The bubbles that form cause the bread to expand.

Because the reaction begins as soon as the ingredients are mixed, you want to take advantage of this by baking the bread right away.

Finally, if you are making **free-form loaves, rolls or buns** on a baking sheet, shape them approximately the height you want them to be, prior to placing them in the oven. Do not flatten the rolls or buns on the sheet before baking.

Now, let's discuss how to get the best rise from your **Yeast Breads**...

There are five recipes in this book that include an <u>optional</u> yeast preparation. We included these recipes based on popular demand. Many people simply love the old-world flavor of yeast breads. Of course, yeast also helps these breads to rise.

Part of the rise in yeast breads is the result of fermentation. As the yeast feeds on carbohydrates, carbon dioxide "bubbles" are formed – expanding the bread and creating the soft, spongy texture we all know and love.

However, because these breads are very low in carbohydrates, there is virtually nothing for the yeast to consume. That is why these five recipes call for a small amount of **honey** or **maple syrup**. *But wait a second*, you ask...

HOW ARE THESE RECIPES "KETO" IF SOME HAVE SUGAR?!

First, it's important to understand only a teaspoon or two of these ingredients are used in these particular recipes. We include just enough fermentable substrate for the yeast. As the yeast transforms the energy in the carbohydrates, the mixture begins to foam. This is evidence that the sugars are being consumed by the yeast – so they won't be consumed by your body.

Once the mixture has "bloomed", the small amount of sugar is almost entirely consumed and very little remains in the final product. The end result is a bread that is still VERY low in carbohydrates and fully compliant with the ketogenic macronutrient ratio.

For example, if you follow the "Yeast Preparation" for our *Keto French Bread*, you will add two teaspoons of maple syrup or honey to the yeast mixture. The final nutritional analysis of this bread reveals just 5g carbohydrate (and 2g net carbohydrate, after fiber is deducted).

By measure of calories, this bread consists of 79 percent healthy fat, 15 percent protein and just 6 percent carbohydrates. These nutritional attributes are well within the range of what is considered "ketogenic."

However, please keep in mind that the "Yeast Preparation" is optional. If you avoid yeast or if you do not wish to add any sugars to your bread (even if they are transformed before you consume them) you can simply leave these ingredients out of the recipe and skip the steps that involve the yeast mixture.

You can also swap the honey or maple syrup for a **pre-biotic fiber**, like **inulin**. This provides the yeast a source of carbohydrate to consume, without using a form of sugar.

And of course, if you're familiar with baking bread, you know that yeast breads need time to rise *before* they are baked, so let's discuss...

HOW TO ACHIEVE THE PERFECT "PROOFING" ENVIRONMENT

As opposed to **Quick Breads**, which should go in the oven right away, **Yeast Breads** need time to "proof" before baking. During this time (and given the proper environment), the yeast will feed on the carbohydrates. Gasses will form and the bread will rise.

So, let's cover some of the basics of creating the perfect proofing environment to achieve the optimal rise from your yeast breads.

First, ensure that you are using **active dry yeast.** We recommend you use an organic product that has not been genetically modified. And you should not use "instant" or "rapid rise" yeast, as these products may not produce the same results.

Yeast thrives in a warm (not hot) environment.

Your bread will rise faster and more completely when all your ingredients are at room temperature. If any are stored in the refrigerator or freezer, measure these ingredients a few hours before baking and make sure they have reached room temperature before you begin.

You also want to be sure that the water you add is warm. The ideal range is from **105°–115°F (41°–46°C).** If the water is too cool, the yeast will not "bloom." If it is too hot, it will kill the organisms. So warm your water on the stove or in the microwave. Then test the temperature with a thermometer before adding your yeast and sweetener (the food source for the yeast). Stir with a warm spoon, cover and set aside.

Within minutes, the yeast should begin to foam. If it does NOT foam, start over. This could indicate that the yeast is not active. If you follow these instructions carefully and the mixture fails to bloom a second time, you may need to buy a new package of yeast.

Once the wet yeast mixture has been added to the dry ingredients and mixed, set the dough in a warm place to rest. In this case, the temperature should be **80°– 90°F (27°–32°C).** The temperature should not go over 100°F (38°C) during this stage.

If it is winter or your house is very cool, you will need to create a warm environment for the bread to rest in the pan. One option is to put it in the oven with the light bulb on. The small amount of heat from the bulb should keep the oven at just the right temperature.

You could also place the dough in the pan and set the pan over a warm towel (carefully heat a wet towel in the microwave until warm). Then cover the pan with a kitchen towel. Finally, you could also place your pan on a trivet, which sits on top of a countertop oven (or toaster oven). Set the oven to "warm" and the rising heat should keep the dough in the right temperature range.

A FEW MORE TIPS FOR INCREASING THE "HEIGHT" OF YOUR BREADS

I encourage you to make the recipes in this book exactly as they are presented the first time. After you have established the baseline, feel free to experiment. If there is a recipe you enjoy, and you'd like to get a bit more "height" here are a few things you might try...

If you'd like to "double" a recipe to get more volume, you might need to use a different-sized pan. Keep in mind the rule of thumb that the dough or batter should come three-quarters up the side of the pan before baking. Doubling the recipe might also require adjusting the baking time (refer to the section below to know when your bread is done).

You might also increase the sweetener. This will provide more carbohydrates for the yeast to feed on. However, it may also provide more carbs for your body to feed on if these sugars are not fully consumed!

You might also consider replacing the water with **carbonated water**. Carbonated liquids contain carbon dioxide bubbles. This can help boost the volume in bread. You can try this for any recipe that calls for water – not just those that include yeast.

Finally, you might add a few grams of **powdered ascorbic acid (vitamin C)** to the dry ingredients. Yeast thrives in an acidic environment and this can help to promote greater volume. Ascorbic acid also acts as a natural preservative, which may extend shelf-life.

Now, let's answer some common questions and cover other important tips for **baking better breads**...

HOW DO YOU KNOW WHEN YOUR BREADS ARE DONE?

Most of the breads you bake will turn a nice golden-brown color when they are done. But the color on top is not always an indication that the center has finished baking.

You can also check for doneness by inserting a toothpick near the center. When the bread is cooked through, the toothpick should come out clean.

However, the best way to ensure your bread has finished baking is to insert an **instant read thermometer** into the center. For most of these recipes, the internal temperature should reach **205° – 210°F (96°- 99°C)**.

It is also important to know that every oven is different. And many are not properly calibrated. It is not unusual for a residential oven to be off by 50°F (10°C) or more. And temperature variations can make a big difference in baking. If you bake bread in an oven that is too hot, the outside will be done before the inside has a chance to develop the necessary structure.

So be sure to check your bread through the glass during the last ten minutes or so. Make sure the top is not getting too done. And when it's time to take it out, use an instant read thermometer to make sure the inside has reached the correct temperature.

COOLING YOUR BREAD AFTER BAKING

Once you smell the delightful aroma coming from your oven, your first temptation will be to take your bread out as soon as it is done and cut off a slice to enjoy with warm melted butter.

Please don't remove it from the pan too soon. It still needs some time to set and you don't want your bread to fall. Of course, you don't want to leave it in the pan too long either. If you do, condensation can form. And nobody likes soggy bread.

Allow it to cool in the pan for 10-15 minutes. Then remove it from the pan and set it on a wire rack, so that air can circulate around it. There are a few breads in this book you should allow to **cool completely** before slicing. Otherwise, you may compress the center before it has a chance to set – and the bread could end up "gummy."

Specific instructions for cooling each bread are included with the recipes.

STORING & FREEZING YOUR BREAD

Once your bread has cooled and the residual moisture has dissipated, store it in an airtight container. You can store it on the counter, but if you keep it in the refrigerator it will last longer.

And in case you want to make a few batches and save some for later, all of these breads freeze perfectly. As long as there is no freezer burn, there should be no difference in the taste or texture when thawed.

The best way to freeze your bread is to let it cool completely. Then wrap whole loaves, rolls or slices individually in plastic freezer wrap. That way they will not freeze together. And wrap tightly so that most of the air is removed. Once the bread is wrapped, place the wraps in a zip-top freezer bag. Then store in the freezer.

As long as you take these steps to prevent frost and freezer burn, your bread will keep almost indefinitely.

EGG WASH VS. WATER SPRAY VS. OIL DRIZZLE

Many bakers like to spray their dough with water, drizzle with oil or brush with a whisked egg yolk before baking. Each of these methods has different benefits and will produce different results.

An egg wash will add a glossy golden sheen to the outside of the bread. It is important to note that using an egg wash will also make the crust a bit more flexible and less crusty.

If you want a "hard roll" crust, opt for a water spray. Or bake your bread on a pizza stone with a ceramic ramekin of water on the rack underneath. While this method helps to produce crustier bread, it will not have any sheen.

An oil drizzle is another method for giving your bread a bit of sheen and a chewy crust. I prefer avocado oil, which has a higher flash point (500°F / 260°C) than olive oil, making it less prone to oxidation during baking.

SHOULD YOU MAKE ANY ALTITUDE ADJUSTMENTS?

All of these recipes were developed in the Wasatch mountains of Northern Utah. Our elevation here is around 5,300 feet. Thousands of readers have made our bread recipes over the years, achieving excellent results near sea level and in the mountains.

So, unless you live at a **very high elevation**, there is no need to make adjustments.

If you do live at a significant elevation, you may need to adjust the baking time, temperature or the amount of liquid. However, we suggest you follow the recipe exactly the first time. Just be sure to watch carefully and check early to see if it is done. Take notes on your results and consider making adjustments the next time you bake.

There are also many articles and tables online with small, simple adjustments you can make to get the best results. But for most, this will be unnecessary. Just follow the recipes exactly, and your results should look just like those pictured.

ALLERGIES, INTOLERANCES & HEALTHY SUBSTITUTIONS

The concept of an allergic reaction is nothing new. It has been discussed in medical literature since the early 1900s. But the massive numbers of people suffering from food allergies and intolerances today is a new phenomenon. We are experiencing an "allergy epidemic."

Many experts believe our consumption of wheat has a lot to do with it. And the protein we call "gluten" is only part of the story. A study published in *Plant Physiology* showed that modern wheat is capable of producing at least 23,788 unique proteins.[1] And any one of these is capable of causing an inflammatory reaction in the gut.

Chronic digestive inflammation can lead to leaky gut – a condition where the gut wall is compromised. When this critical barrier is breached, harmful compounds and undigested food particles can "leak" into the bloodstream.

This fuels a continuous state of low-grade inflammation. It can also trigger the immune system and is implicated in the rise of allergies, autoimmune illness, chronic fatigue and a range of illnesses.

The great news is that by choosing **Keto Breads** you can now enjoy all the delicious bread you want – without the harmful effects of grain. And if you do suffer from leaky gut, avoiding grain is the number-one step you can take to heal and restore your digestive system.

Many people find that healing their gut causes allergies to go away. That is exactly what happened to me. When I was first tested, I had nearly two dozen allergies and intolerances, ranging from mild to severe. When I was tested years later, only a few mild intolerances remained.

So I am well aware of these issues. And whenever possible, we have included ingredient substitutions for the benefit of those with food allergies and intolerances. In this section, we discuss **substitutions for dairy**, **tree nuts**, **coconut** and **eggs**.

DAIRY

As you probably know, a lot of keto recipes rely on dairy. That is not the case in this book. The majority of recipes in **Keto Breads** are dairy free or can be made dairy free by substituting coconut oil (or any fat that is solid at room temperature) in place of butter.

However, there are five recipes in the book that call for cheddar, mozzarella, cream cheese or sour cream. These ingredients serve an important purpose in the recipe and cannot be left out, while achieving the same results. We have also included several recipes for **Heathy Substitutions** at the end of the book, featuring **Dairy-Free Sour Cream** and **Paleo "Cream" Cheese**, if you'd like to substitute these ingredients with non-dairy options.

NUTS

Most recipes in this book use almond flour. We love this ingredient for the taste, texture and properties it can impart. But we also know some people must avoid nuts.

If you are nut free, you can substitute **sunflower seed flour** – gram for gram – in any recipe that calls for almond flour. There are several ready-milled brands on Amazon. And most health food stores carry the product.

You can also make your own from whole seeds. Using a food processor or blender, add raw (or soaked and dehydrated) sunflower seeds to the vessel. Pulse until you reach a flour-like consistency. Be very careful not to over-grind. There is a fine line between turning nuts and seeds into "flour"... and turning them into "butter."

It may help to sift the flour through a mesh strainer. Add any larger pieces back to the blender until you have created a fine texture. One cup (240 ml) of sunflower seeds yields a little less than one cup of flour.

And because the oils in nuts and seeds can go rancid, it is best to make this flour in small batches and use within a short period of time.

You may also store the milled seeds in an airtight container in the refrigerator or freezer.

When using sunflower seed flour with baking soda, you may notice a light green color in the final product. This is because sunflower seeds have high amounts of chlorogenic acid (which happens to be a very healthy antioxidant). In the presence of heat – and with the addition of baking soda or baking powder – this compound will turn green.

It is perfectly safe to eat, so don't worry about that. However, you should be able to reduce the reaction by adding an additional teaspoon or two of apple cider vinegar (or lemon juice if you prefer).

EGGS

Eggs are a nearly-perfect superfood… unless you have an egg allergy!

Unfortunately, most commercial egg replacers contain soy protein and wheat gluten – two allergenic ingredients in their own right. However, there are ingredients that can approximate the properties of eggs.

If you are sensitive to chicken eggs, consider trying **duck eggs**. Some people who have an intolerance or allergy to chicken eggs do not have the same problem with duck eggs. Obviously, take this approach with caution if you have a serious allergy.

If you cannot tolerate duck eggs, my next preferred substitute is a **"gel egg"** using your choice of **gelatin, ground flax seeds** or **ground chia seeds**.

You can use these ingredients to create a gel that can act as a binder and source of moisture. Here is the formula for creating flax or chia "eggs":

- 1 Tbsp. milled flax seeds + 3 Tbsp. hot water = 1 egg
- 1 Tbsp. milled chia seeds + 3 Tbsp. hot water = 1 egg

Simply mix the ground seeds with the hot water and whisk to combine. Let the mixture sit for 20 minutes, while whisking occasionally, until a gel forms.

If you would prefer to use gelatin, here is the formula:

- 1 Tbsp. grass-fed gelatin + 1 Tbsp. warm water + 2 Tbsp. hot water = 1 egg

Mix the gelatin and 1 Tbsp. of warm water. It will swell slightly. Then pour 2 Tbsp. of hot water over the mixture and whisk vigorously. The gelatin will dissolve and turn into a sticky paste. Allow the gelatin "egg" to sit for two to three minutes before using.

Use any of the gels above just as you would use eggs.

As you might expect, the resulting bread will not be as fluffy as it would be otherwise. If your recipe turns out flatter than you want it to be, add an extra teaspoon of baking powder (not baking soda) to the recipe to help the bread rise.

As a rule, the fewer eggs a recipe calls for, the easier they will be to replace. If a recipe calls for three eggs, your results will probably be poor. On the other hand, if a recipe calls for just one egg, it is serving as a binder and should be an easy replacement.

Here are some additional formulas for replacing an egg. Although, please keep in mind that some of these will add some carbs to your bread and it may no longer be "keto."

- 2 Tbsp. arrowroot flour = 1 egg
- 2 Tbsp. potato starch = 1 egg
- 1 mashed banana = 1 egg
- ¼ cup unsweetened apple sauce = 1 egg
- ¼ cup organic plain yogurt, whipped = 1 egg
- 2 Tbsp. water + 1 Tbsp. oil + 1 tsp. baking powder, mixed well = 1 egg
- ¼ cup cooked pumpkin or winter squash = 1 egg

And now, without further ado, let's bake some bread!

---

1. Vandepoele K, Van de Peer Y. Exploring the plant transcriptome through phylogenetic profiling. Plant Physiology. 2005 Jan;137(1):31-42.

Loaf
Breads

SESAME-ONION SANDWICH BREAD

This savory loaf is chewy, dense and flavorful — and just right for piling high with grass-fed roast beef, sliced turkey or chicken salad to create the perfect grain-free sandwich.

YIELD: One 8" x 4" (20 x 10 cm) loaf (16 slices)

INGREDIENTS

DRY INGREDIENTS

- ¾ cup sifted coconut flour (80 g)
- ¼ cup ground golden flaxseed (28 g)
- 2 Tbsp. tapioca flour (13 g)
- ½ tsp. baking soda (2.5 g)
- 1 tsp. non-aluminum baking powder (5 g)
- ½ tsp. sea salt (2.5 g)
- 1 tsp. onion powder (5 g)
- 2 tsp. organic psyllium husk powder (6 g)
- 2 Tbsp. sesame seeds (14 g) + 1 Tbsp. sesame seeds (7g) for topping

Ingredients continued...

WET INGREDIENTS

- 7 pastured eggs (350 g)
- ½ cup virgin coconut oil, melted (120 ml)
- 2 Tbsp. organic cultured sour cream or *Dairy-Free Sour Cream* (page 110) (30 ml)

DIRECTIONS

1. Grease or line the bottom of an 8" x 4" (20 x 10 cm) loaf pan with parchment.

2. Preheat oven to 350°F (177°C).

3. In a small bowl, combine the dry ingredients (except for the reserved sesame seeds).

4. In a medium bowl, beat the eggs, sour cream and coconut oil.

5. Stir dry ingredients into wet to combine. The batter will be thick and sticky.

6. Spread into pan and pat down to create an even top. Sprinkle with sesame seeds.

7. Transfer to oven and bake 40-45 minutes or until a toothpick comes out clean and loaf is golden.

8. Cool bread in the pan for 10-15 minutes. Then transfer to a wire rack, until cooled completely. Store in an airtight container.

NUTRITION INFORMATION

140 calories, 12 g fat, 8 g saturated fat, 2 g monounsaturated fat, 1 g polyunsaturated fat, 93 mg cholesterol, 5 g carbohydrate, 3 g NET carbs, 0 g sugar alcohols, 1 g sugar, 3 g fiber, 4 g protein, 88 mg potassium, 86 mg phosphorous, 153 mg sodium, 16 mg magnesium

MACRONUTRIENT RATIO

79% FAT ■ 13% PROTEIN ■ 8% CARBOHYDRATE

HEARTY SANDWICH BREAD

If you love the dense and nutty nature of whole grain bread, this loaf is sure to please. Feel free to add a tablespoon of sesame, sunflower or poppy seeds for a more toothsome texture.

YIELD: One 7.5" x 3.5" (19 x 9 cm) loaf (16 slices)

INGREDIENTS

DRY INGREDIENTS

- ½ cup sifted coconut flour (50 g)
- ½ cup ground golden flaxseed (50 g)
- 1 tsp. baking soda (5 g)
- ½ tsp. sea salt (2.5 g)
- 1 tsp. tapioca flour (2.5 g)
- ½ tsp. cream of tartar (1.5 g)
- 1 Tbsp. + 1 tsp. organic psyllium husk powder (12 g)
- 1 Tbsp. ground caraway seeds (6 g) optional for "rye" bread

Ingredients continued...

WET INGREDIENTS

- 6 pastured eggs (300 g)
- 1 Tbsp. organic apple cider vinegar (15 ml)
- 2 tsp. virgin coconut oil, melted (10 ml)
- 2 Tbsp. organic coconut milk (full fat) (30 ml)

DIRECTIONS

1. Preheat oven to 325°F (163°C).

2. Grease the bottom of a 7.5" x 3.5" (19 x 9 cm) loaf pan or line with parchment paper. This bread should rise to a little less than three inches (7 cm).

3. In a small bowl, combine the dry ingredients.

4. In a medium bowl, beat the wet ingredients.

5. Stir dry ingredients into wet to combine. The batter will be thick and sticky, like oatmeal.

6. Spread into pan. Transfer to oven and bake 40-45 minutes or until a toothpick comes out clean and loaf is golden.

7. Cool bread in the pan for 10-15 minutes. Then transfer to a wire rack, until cooled completely. Store in an airtight container.

NUTRITION INFORMATION

72 calories, 5 g fat, 2 g saturated fat, 1 g monounsaturated fat, 1 g polyunsaturated fat, 79 mg cholesterol, 4 g carbohydrate, 1 g NET carbs, 0 g sugar alcohols, 0.5 g sugar, 3 g fiber, 4 g protein, 66 mg potassium, 58 mg phosphorous, 187 mg sodium, 16 mg magnesium

MACRONUTRIENT RATIO

70% FAT ■ 23% PROTEIN ■ 8% CARBOHYDRATE

ALMOND BUTTER BREAD

This bread is slightly sweet, with a soft crumb and delicate texture – perfect for lightly toasting or piling on your favorite keto-friendly sandwich fillings.

YIELD: One 8" x 4" (20 x 10 cm) loaf (16 slices)

INGREDIENTS

DRY INGREDIENTS

- ¼ cup almond flour (33 g)
- 3 Tbsp. tapioca flour (18 g)
- ½ tsp. baking soda (2.5 g)
- ½ tsp. sea salt (2.5 g)
- 1 tsp. non-aluminum baking powder (5 g)

WET INGREDIENTS

- ¾ cup almond butter (180 ml)
- ¼ cup virgin coconut oil, melted (60 ml)
- 4 pastured eggs (200 g)
- 1 Tbsp. organic apple cider vinegar (15 ml)

DIRECTIONS

1. Preheat oven to 350°F (177°C).

2. Grease an 8" x 4" (20 x 10 cm) loaf pan.

3. Place a parchment sling in the greased pan, covering the bottom and extending over the edges.

4. In a small bowl, combine the dry ingredients.

5. Add the wet ingredients to a high-powered blender or food processor. Blend on medium speed to combine. Add dry ingredients. Continue to blend until smooth. Batter will be thick and sticky.

6. Pour batter into pan. Transfer to oven and bake 30-35 minutes or until edges pull away and a toothpick comes out clean.

7. Cool bread in the pan for 10-15 minutes. Then transfer to a wire rack, until cooled completely. Store in an airtight container.

NUTRITION INFORMATION

129 calories, 12 g fat, 4 g saturated fat, 5 g monounsaturated fat, 2 g polyunsaturated fat, 53 mg cholesterol, 4 g carbohydrate, 2 g NET carbs, 0 g sugar alcohols, 1 g sugar, 2 g fiber, 5 g protein, 29 mg potassium, 24 mg phosphorous, 95 mg sodium, 11 mg magnesium

MACRONUTRIENT RATIO

79% FAT ■ 14% PROTEIN ■ 7% CARBOHYDRATE

CLASSIC SANDWICH LOAF

This soft and chewy bread scratches the itch for the All-American slice. Delicious when toasted and slathered with butter, it also makes the perfect French toast.

YIELD: One 7.5" X 3.5" (19 x 9 cm) loaf (12 slices)

INGREDIENTS

DRY INGREDIENTS

- ¾ cup almond flour (80 g)
- 3 Tbsp. coconut flour (20 g)
- 1 tsp. baking soda (5 g)
- ¼ tsp. sea salt (1.3 g)
- 3 tsp. organic psyllium husk powder (9 g)

WET INGREDIENTS

- ¼ cup hot water (60 ml)
- 3 pastured eggs + 1 egg white (180 g)
- 2 Tbsp. organic apple cider vinegar (30 ml)

DIRECTIONS

1. Preheat oven to 350°F (177°C).

2. Grease a 7.5" x 3.5" (19 x 9 cm) loaf pan.

3. Place a parchment sling in the greased pan, covering the bottom and extending over the edges. This bread should rise to about two inches (5 cm).

4. In a small bowl, combine the dry ingredients.

5. In another bowl, whisk the eggs, egg white and apple cider vinegar. Add the dry ingredients and stir until combined.

6. Pour in hot water and stir vigorously. Batter will be thick and sticky, like oatmeal.

7. Spread into prepared pan. Transfer to oven. Bake 35 minutes or until a toothpick comes out clean.

8. Cool bread in the pan for 10-15 minutes. Then transfer to a wire rack, until cooled completely. Store in an airtight container.

NUTRITION INFORMATION

60 calories, 4 g fat, 1 g saturated fat, 2 g monounsaturated fat, 1 g polyunsaturated fat, 53 mg cholesterol, 3 g carbohydrate, 1 g NET carbs, 0 g sugar alcohols, 0.4 g sugar, 2 g fiber, 3 g protein, 70 mg potassium, 24 mg phosphorous, 182 mg sodium, 20 mg magnesium

MACRONUTRIENT RATIO

70% FAT ■ 23% PROTEIN ■ 7% CARBOHYDRATE

SUMMER ZUCCHINI BREAD

With the same dense, moist texture of traditional zucchini bread, our low-carb version takes a savory spin. For a sweet bread, add a quarter cup of powdered erythritol, plus liquid stevia (to taste).

YIELD: One 7.5" x 3.5" (19 x 9 cm) loaf (16 slices)

INGREDIENTS

DRY INGREDIENTS

- 1 cup coconut flour (100 g)
- 1 tsp. baking soda (5 g)
- ½ tsp. sea salt (2.5 g)

WET INGREDIENTS

- 1½ cups finely shredded organic zucchini (240 g)
- ½ cup virgin coconut oil, melted (120 ml)
- 6 pastured eggs (300 g)
- 1 Tbsp. organic apple cider vinegar (15 ml)
- 1 Tbsp. lemon juice (15 ml) + 2 tsp. organic lemon zest (5 g)

DIRECTIONS

1. Preheat the oven to 350°F (177°C).

2. Grease a 7.5" x 3.5" (19 x 9 cm) loaf pan.

3. Place a parchment sling in the greased pan, covering the bottom and extending over the edges.

4. In a medium bowl, whisk the dry ingredients.

5. In a large bowl, whisk the eggs, melted coconut oil, vinegar, lemon juice and zest.

6. Whisk the coconut flour mixture into the egg-oil mixture until well combined. Stir in the finely shredded zucchini. Mix well to distribute throughout the thick batter.

7. Scrape batter into the prepared pan and press down to create a flat, even top.

8. Transfer to oven and bake 55-60 minutes or until a toothpick comes out clean.

9. Cool completely before slicing. Store cooled bread in an airtight container.

NUTRITION INFORMATION

112 calories, 10 g fat, 7 g saturated fat, 1 g monounsaturated fat, 0.4 g polyunsaturated fat, 79 mg cholesterol, 4 g carbohydrate, 2 g NET carbs, 0 g sugar alcohols, 1 g sugar, 2 g fiber, 3 g protein, 59 mg potassium, 41 mg phosphorous, 191 mg sodium, 5 mg magnesium

MACRONUTRIENT RATIO

82% FAT ■ 12% PROTEIN ■ 6% CARBOHYDRATE

BETTER BANANA BREAD

This slightly sweet loaf will remind you of the version Grandma used to make. Only our rendition is grain free and very low in carbs and sugar!

YIELD: One 7.5" x 3.5" (19 x 9 cm) loaf (16 slices)

INGREDIENTS

DRY INGREDIENTS

- ½ cup coconut flour (55 g)
- ½ cup almond flour (50 g)
- ½ tsp. baking soda (2.5 g)
- ¼ tsp. sea salt (1.3 g)
- ⅛ tsp. stevia extract (0.5 ml) or 15-20 drops liquid stevia (optional)

WET INGREDIENTS

- ½ cup virgin coconut oil, melted (120 ml)
- 4 pastured eggs (200 g)
- 2 tsp. organic vanilla extract (10 ml)

FOLD IN

- 1 cup mashed bananas (240 ml)
- 2 oz. chopped walnuts (57 g) (optional)

DIRECTIONS

1. Preheat the oven to 350°F (177°C).

2. Grease a 7.5" x 3.5" (19 x 9 cm) loaf pan.

3. Place a parchment sling in the greased pan, covering the bottom and extending over the edges.

4. In a medium bowl, whisk the coconut flour, almond flour, baking soda, sea salt.

5. In a large bowl, whisk the eggs, melted coconut oil and vanilla.

6. Add the dry ingredients to the wet and mix well, using a hand-held mixer or a silicone spatula.

7. Fold in the bananas and nuts (if using).

8. Scrape the thick batter into the prepared pan and smooth the top.

9. Transfer to oven and bake 45 minutes or until golden brown and a toothpick inserted into the center comes out clean.

10. Store cooled bread in an airtight container.

NUTRITION INFORMATION

145 calories, 13 g fat, 7g saturated fat, 3 g monounsaturated fat, 1 g polyunsaturated fat, 53mg cholesterol, 6g carbohydrate, 4 g NET carbs, 0 g sugar alcohols, 2 g sugar, 2g fiber, 3 g protein, 99 mg potassium, 35 mg phosphorous, 101 mg sodium, 18 mg magnesium

MACRONUTRIENT RATIO

80% FAT ■ 9% PROTEIN ■ 11% CARBOHYDRATE

"CORN" BREAD

This dense buttery, golden loaf develops crisp edges when cooked in a cast iron pan. For flavor closest to cornbread, use pastured ghee or butter (not oil).

YIELD: One 7.5" x 3.5" (19 x 9 cm) loaf or 8" (20 cm) cast iron pan (12 slice

INGREDIENTS

DRY INGREDIENTS

- 6 Tbsp. coconut flour (38 g)
- ¼ cup tapioca flour (33 g)
- ¼ tsp. baking soda (1.3 g)
- ¼ tsp. sea salt (1.3 g)
- ½ tsp. cream of tartar (1.6 g)
- ½ tsp. psyllium husk powder (2 g) (optional, but reduces crumble)

WET INGREDIENTS

- 4 pastured eggs (200 g)
- ¼ cup pastured ghee, butter or virgin coconut oil, melted (60 ml)
- 1 tsp. organic apple cider vinegar (5 ml)
- 1-15 drops liquid stevia (optional, but adds traditional cornbread sweetness)

FOLD IN

- ½ can (196 g) *Native Forest Organic Baby Corn*, finely chopped

DIRECTIONS

1. Preheat the oven to 350°F (177°C).

2. Grease a 7.5" x 3.5" (19 x 9 cm) loaf pan.

3. Place a parchment sling in the greased pan, covering the bottom and extending over the edges.

4. In a medium bowl, whisk the dry ingredients.

5. Add the eggs, melted butter, ghee or coconut oil and vinegar, as well as stevia, if using. Blend on medium speed to combine.

6. Pour the dry ingredients into the wet. Mix on medium-low speed for 30 seconds to fully combine. Let the batter stand for 1 minute to thicken. Stir in the chopped baby corn.

7. Scrape batter into the prepared pan. Smooth the top with your spatula or by gently rapping the pan on the counter.

8. Transfer to oven and bake 30 minutes or until golden and a toothpick comes out clean. Cool completely before slicing.

9. Store cooled bread in an airtight container.

FOR CAST-IRON CORNBREAD: Prepare batter as directed. Pour into a lightly greased 8" (20 cm) cast-iron pan and bake until bread is firm to the touch and a toothpick comes out clean, about 25 minutes.

NUTRITION INFORMATION

95 calories, 8g fat, 6 g saturated fat, 1 g monounsaturated fat, 0.3 g polyunsaturated fat, 71 mg cholesterol, 3 g carbohydrate, 3 g NET carbs, 0 g sugar alcohols, 0.4 g sugar, 1 g fiber, 2 g protein, 53 mg potassium, 38 mg phosphorous, 122 mg sodium, 5 mg magnesium

MACRONUTRIENT RATIO

79% FAT ■ 10% PROTEIN ■ 11% CARBOHYDRATE

KETO PROTEIN BREAD

With its airy pockets and butter-loving nooks, this crispy-crusted golden loaf is perfect for sopping up the yolks from a breakfast of farm-fresh eggs.

YIELD: One 7.5" x 3.5" (19 x 9 cm) loaf (16 slices)

INGREDIENTS

DRY INGREDIENTS

- 2½ Tbsp. psyllium husk powder (22 g)
- 1 scoop plain whey protein or unflavored *Ancient Nutrition Bone Broth Protein* (15 g)
- ¼ tsp. sea salt (1.3 g)
- 2 tsp. non-aluminum baking powder (10 g)

WET INGREDIENTS

- 5½ ounces organic cream cheese, room temperature (156 g)
- 3 large pastured eggs (150 g)
- 1 Tbsp. organic apple cider vinegar (15 ml)

ADD IN & TOPPING

- 1 ounce pumpkin seeds (28 g)
- ½ Tbsp. chia seeds
- 1 tsp. sesame seeds (2 g)

KETO *Breads*

DIRECTIONS

1. Preheat oven to 325°F (163°C).

2. Line a 7.5" x 3.5" (19 x 9 cm) pan with unbleached parchment paper. Ensure cream cheese is at room temperature.

3. In a medium bowl, add soft cream cheese and beat with an electric mixer on high to cream. Add eggs, one at a time, beating after each addition. Pour in apple cider vinegar and beat again.

4. In a small bowl, whisk together the psyllium husk powder, sea salt, baking powder and bone broth protein powder.

5. Pour dry ingredients into wet and mix on high speed to combine. Stir in pumpkin seeds and chia.

6. Scrape batter into the prepared loaf pan. Top with sesame seeds.

7. Transfer to oven and bake for 35 minutes or until golden brown and a toothpick inserted into the center comes out clean.

8. Cool completely before slicing.

NUTRITION INFORMATION

70 calories, 5 g fat, 3 g saturated fat, 2 g monounsaturated fat, 1 g polyunsaturated fat, 50 mg cholesterol, 2 g carbohydrate, 1 g NET carbs, 0 g sugar alcohols, 0.1 g sugar, 1 g fiber, 5 g protein, 111 mg potassium, 96 mg phosphorous, 88 mg sodium, 13 mg magnesium

MACRONUTRIENT RATIO

72% FAT ■ 22% PROTEIN ■ 6% CARBOHYDRATE

CASHEW SOURDOUGH BREAD

*This cultured probiotic bread has a soft crumb, a crisp golden top...
and the tangy taste of sourdough we all know and love.*

YIELD: One 7.5" x 3.5" (19 x 9 cm) loaf (16 slices)

INGREDIENTS

DRY INGREDIENTS

- 10 ounces raw cashews (285 g)
- ½ cup filtered water (120 ml)
- Probiotic powder (to equal 30 billion colony forming units)

SECONDARY INGREDIENTS

- 2 pastured eggs, separated + 1 egg yolk + 1 tsp. water (for egg wash)
- 1 Tbsp. water (15 ml)
- ½ tsp. baking soda (2.5 g)
- ½ tsp. sea salt (2.5 g)
- 2 tsp. psyllium husk powder (6 g) (optional, but makes a chewier bread)

DIRECTIONS

1. Make the culture. Place the ½ cup (120 ml) of filtered water and 10 ounces (285 g) of cashews into a high-powered blender or food processor. Blend until very smooth. Transfer to a deep non-reactive container and stir in probiotic powder. Cover the container. Place in an oven with the oven light turned on. The goal is to keep the cashew culture between 100 –105°F (38–41°C) for 12-24 hours. (The longer it stands the tangier your bread will be).

2. Preheat oven to 300°F (149°C). Lightly grease the 7.5" x 3.5" (19 x 9 cm) pan and line it with parchment paper, extending over all sides of the tin.

3. Add the egg yolks and 1 Tbsp. (15 ml) water to the cultured cashew mixture. Beat with a hand mixer until smooth. Mix in the baking soda and salt.

4. Using clean, dry beaters beat the egg whites until soft peaks form. Gently fold the egg whites into the cashew mixture until they are no longer visible.

5. Pour the batter into prepared loaf pan. Prepare the egg wash by mixing the egg yolk with 1 tsp. (5 ml) water. Using a pastry brush, gently brush the egg wash on top of the batter.

6. Transfer to oven and bake for 40 minutes, or until a toothpick inserted into the center comes out dry. Increase the oven temperature to 375°F (191°C). Bake for an additional 5-10 minutes, or until the top is golden and crusty.

7. Remove from the oven and cool in the pan for 10-15 minutes. Then transfer to a wire rack. Cool this bread completely before slicing. Store in an airtight container.

NUTRITION INFORMATION

110 calories, 9g fat, 2 g saturated fat, 5 g monounsaturated fat, 2 g polyunsaturated fat, 40 mg cholesterol, 6 g carbohydrate, 5 g NET carbs, 0 g sugar alcohols, 1 g sugar, 1 g fiber, 4 g protein, 126 mg potassium, 120 mg phosphorous, 120 mg sodium, 52 mg magnesium

MACRONUTRIENT RATIO

68% FAT ■ 15% PROTEIN ■ 17% CARBOHYDRATE

REAL-DEAL KETO BREAD

This may be the only keto bread recipe you'll ever need. It rises — and tastes — just like "real" bread. And its sturdy composition, firm crust and authentic yeast-bread flavor make it the perfect choice for sandwiches, toast, French toast and more!

YIELD: One 7.5" x 3.5" (19 x 9 cm) loaf (16 slices)

INGREDIENTS

LEAVENING INGREDIENTS

- ½ cup filtered water (120 ml)
- 2 tsp. yeast (6 g)
- 2 tsp. maple syrup or honey (10 ml)*

WET INGREDIENTS

- 3 large pastured eggs (150 g)
- ¼ cup grass-fed butter or coconut oil, melted (56 g)
- ¼ cup organic yogurt, sour cream, coconut cream or *Dairy-Free Sour Cream* (page 110) (60 g)
- 1 Tbsp. organic apple cider vinegar (15 ml)

Ingredients continued...

DRY INGREDIENTS

- 1½ cups almond flour (150 g)
- ⅔ cup golden flax meal (80 g)
- 2 Tbsp. psyllium husk powder (18 g)

- 2 tsp. non-aluminum baking powder (10 g)
- 1 tsp. sea salt (5 g)
- ¼ tsp. cream of tartar (0.75 g)
- 2 tsp. grass-fed beef gelatin (6 g)

DIRECTIONS

1. Line a 7.5" x 3.5" (19 x 9 cm) pan with unbleached parchment paper. Add the yeast and sweetener* (maple syrup or honey) to a large bowl. Heat water to 105°F - 110°F (41°C - 43°C) and pour over yeast. Cover with a kitchen towel to bloom for 7 minutes. If yeast does not produce foam, start over.

2. Mix the dry ingredients in a small bowl.

3. In another bowl, whisk the eggs, vinegar, sour cream and melted butter.

4. Add the wet ingredients into the yeast mixture. Using a hand held mixer, beat to combine. Pour in the dry ingredients and beat on medium to fully combine.

5. Scrape batter into prepared loaf pan. For the largest rise, do not pat batter down. For a smooth top, pat down gently. For a shiny, golden crust, gently brush with egg wash. Cover with a kitchen towel and place in a draft-free area to rise for 50 minutes. Your bread should rise from 1-2 inches.

6. Preheat oven to 350°F (177°C). Transfer risen bread to oven and bake 40-45 minutes or to internal temperature of 205°F (96°C). To prevent over-browning, cover loosely with aluminum foil the last 15 minutes.

7. Cool bread in the pan on a wire rack for 30 minutes. Remove from pan and transfer to wire rack. Cool completely before slicing.

NOTE: Sweetener is used to feed the yeast. Once the yeast blooms, no sweetener remains.

NUTRITION INFORMATION

95 calories, 8g fat, 6 g saturated fat, 1 g monounsaturated fat, 0.3 g polyunsaturated fat, 71 mg cholesterol, 3 g carbohydrate, 3 g NET carbs, 0 g sugar alcohols, 0.4 g sugar, 1 g fiber, 2 g protein, 53 mg potassium, 38 mg phosphorous, 122 mg sodium, 5 mg magnesium

MACRONUTRIENT RATIO

79% FAT ■ 15% PROTEIN ■ 6% CARBOHYDRATE

KETO "RYE" BREAD

This grain-free "rye" bread is divine, when toasted with a pat of butter. It is also the perfect vehicle for corned beef, sauerkraut, Swiss cheese and keto Russian dressing. Say yes to Reubens again!

YIELD: One 7.5" x 3.5" (19 x 9 cm) loaf (16 slices)

INGREDIENTS

LEAVENING INGREDIENTS

- ½ cup brewed chicory or coffee (120 ml)
- 2 tsp. yeast (6 g)
- 2 tsp. molasses (14 g)*

WET INGREDIENTS

- 3 large pastured eggs (150 g)
- ¼ cup grass-fed butter or coconut oil, melted (56 g)
- ¼ cup organic yogurt, sour cream or coconut cream (60 g)

- 1 Tbsp. organic apple cider vinegar (15 ml)

DRY INGREDIENTS

- 1½ cups almond flour (150 g)
- ⅔ cup golden flax meal (80 g)
- 2 Tbsp. psyllium husk powder (18 g)
- 2 Tbsp. organic cocoa powder (12 g)
- 1 Tbsp. caraway seeds (3 g)

Ingredients continued...

- 2 tsp. non-aluminum baking powder (10 g)
- 1 tsp. sea salt (5 g)
- ¼ tsp. cream of tartar (0.75 g)
- 2 tsp. grass-fed beef gelatin (6 g)

DIRECTIONS

1. Line a 7.5" x 3.5" (19 x 9 cm) pan with unbleached parchment paper. Grind the caraway seeds, while reserving some for topping.

2. Add the yeast and molasses to a large bowl. Heat brewed chicory to 105°F - 110°F (41°C - 43°C) and pour over yeast. Cover with a kitchen towel to bloom for 7 minutes. If yeast does not foam, start over.

3. Mix the dry ingredients in a small bowl.

4. In another bowl, whisk the eggs, vinegar, sour cream and melted butter. Add the wet ingredients into the yeast mixture. Using a hand held mixer, beat to combine. Pour in the dry ingredients. Beat on medium speed to fully combine.

5. Scrape batter into prepared loaf pan. For largest rise, do not pat batter down. For a smooth top, pat down gently. For a shiny, golden crust, gently brush with egg wash. Cover with a kitchen towel and place in a draft-free area to rise for 50 minutes. Your bread should rise from 1-2 inches.

6. Preheat oven to 350°F (177°C). Transfer risen bread to oven and bake 40-45 minutes or to internal temperature of 205°F (96°C). To prevent over-browning, cover loosely with aluminum foil in the last 15 minutes.

7. Cool baked bread in the pan on a wire rack for 30 minutes. Then remove from pan and transfer to wire rack to cool completely before slicing.

*NOTE: Sweetener is used to feed the yeast. Once yeast blooms, no sweetener remains.

NUTRITION INFORMATION

138 calories, 11g fat, 3 g saturated fat, 5 g monounsaturated fat, 3 g polyunsaturated fat, 48 mg cholesterol, 6 g carbohydrate, 2 g NET carbs, 0 g sugar alcohols, 1 g sugar, 4 g fiber, 5 g protein, 223 mg potassium, 153 mg phosphorous, 189 mg sodium, 53 mg magnesium

MACRONUTRIENT RATIO

78% FAT ■ 15% PROTEIN ■ 7% CARBOHYDRATE

KETO FRENCH BREAD

Our keto rendition of a French baguette has everything you love (and miss) about this classic French loaf – including the golden crust and soft chewy center – without the grains and carbs!

YIELD: Two 9" x 3" (23 x 8 cm) baguettes (16 servings)

INGREDIENTS

LEAVENING INGREDIENTS

- ½ cup filtered water (120 ml)
- 2 tsp. yeast (6 g)
- 2 tsp. maple syrup or honey (10 ml)*

WET INGREDIENTS

- 3 large pastured eggs (150 g)
- ¼ cup grass-fed butter or coconut oil, melted (56 g)
- ¼ cup organic yogurt, sour cream or coconut cream (60 g)
- 1 Tbsp. organic apple cider vinegar (15 ml)

DRY INGREDIENTS

- 1½ cups almond flour (150 g)
- ⅔ cup golden flax meal (80 g)
- 2 Tbsp. psyllium husk powder (18 g)
- 2 tsp. non-aluminum baking powder (10 g)
- 1 tsp. sea salt (5 g)
- ¼ tsp. cream of tartar (0.75 g)
- 2 tsp. grass-fed beef gelatin (6 g)

DIRECTIONS

1. Line the bottom of a perforated French bread (baguette) pan with strips of unbleached parchment paper.

2. Add the yeast and 2 tsp. sweetener* to a large bowl. Heat water to 105°F - 110°F (41°C - 43°C) and pour over yeast. Cover with a kitchen towel to bloom for 7 minutes.

3. In a small bowl, mix the almond flour, flaxseed powder, psyllium husk powder, baking powder, sea salt, gelatin, and cream of tartar.

4. In another bowl, whisk the eggs, vinegar, sour cream and melted butter.

5. Add the wet ingredients into the yeast mixture. Using a hand held mixer, beat to combine.

6. Pour in the dry ingredients. Beat on medium to fully combine. Let stand 5 minutes to absorb liquid.

7. Divide loose dough in half to make two baguettes. With wet hands, scoop batter onto prepared pan and shape. Gently smooth the surface. For a shiny, golden crust, gently brush with egg wash. Then using a serrated knife or lame cut 3-4 shallow diagonal slashes across the top.

8. Cover with a kitchen towel and place in a draft-free area to rise for 50 minutes. Your dough should rise from 1-2 inches.

9. While dough is rising, preheat oven to 350°F (177°C). Transfer risen dough to oven. Bake 25-35 minutes or to internal temperature of 205°F (96°C). To prevent over-browning, cover loosely with aluminum foil in the last 15 minutes.

10. Cool bread in the pan for 10-15 minutes. Then transfer to a wire rack. Cooled completely before slicing. Store in an airtight container.

NOTE: Sweetener is used to feed the yeast. Once yeast blooms, no sweetener remains.

NUTRITION INFORMATION

134 calories, 11g fat, 3 g saturated fat, 5 g monounsaturated fat, 3 g polyunsaturated fat, 48 mg cholesterol, 5 g carbohydrate, 2 g NET carbs, 0 g sugar alcohols, 1 g sugar, 3 g fiber, 5 g protein, 203 mg potassium,145 mg phosphorous, 188 mg sodium, 48 mg magnesium

MACRONUTRIENT RATIO

79% FAT ■ 15% PROTEIN ■ 6% CARBOHYDRATE

Flatbreads

KETO PITA POCKETS

These soft and flexible pitas are perfect for stuffing with your favorite protein-rich salad for a healthy hand-held lunch. If you're making these for the week ahead, be sure to add the psyllium to help keep the pitas moist and pliable.

YIELD: 2 pita breads (4 pockets)

INGREDIENTS

DRY INGREDIENTS

- ¼ cup almond flour, firmly packed (35 g)
- 2 Tbsp. coconut flour, firmly packed (14 g)
- ⅛ tsp. baking soda (0.6 g)
- ⅛ tsp. sea salt (0.8 g)
- 1 tsp. organic psyllium husk powder (3 g) (optional, but increases pliability and reduces breakage)

WET INGREDIENTS

- ¼ cup hot water (60 ml)
- 1 pastured egg (50 g)
- 1 Tbsp. organic extra virgin olive oil or avocado oil (15 ml)

DIRECTIONS

1. Preheat oven to 350°F (177°C). Prepare a baking sheet with parchment.

2. In a small bowl, combine the dry ingredients.

3. In a medium bowl, combine the wet ingredients, whisking well.

4. Add dry ingredients to wet and mix using a wooden spoon to form a thick batter.

5. Use a ladle to scoop batter by ¼ cupfuls (60 ml) and pour onto parchment-lined pan in circles.

6. Transfer to oven and bake 17-19 minutes.

7. Cool on a wire rack, then cut each circle in half and slice a slit to make a pocket.

8. Store cooled pitas in an airtight container.

NUTRITION INFORMATION

92 calories, 8 g fat, 1 g saturated fat, 5 g monounsaturated fat, 1 g polyunsaturated fat, 53 mg cholesterol, 3 g carbohydrate, 1 g NET carbs, 0 g sugar alcohols, 1 g sugar, 2 g fiber, 3 g protein, 65 mg potassium, 24 mg phosphorous, 161 mg sodium, 19 mg magnesium

MACRONUTRIENT RATIO

81% FAT ■ 14% PROTEIN ■ 5% CARBOHYDRATE

NO GORDITA TORTILLAS

If you're a tortilla lover, you may have tried other Paleo recipes that have a propensity to fall apart mid-bite. We created these sturdy low-carb tortillas to stand up to heaping helpings of whatever you want to stuff inside.

YIELD: Eight 4-inch tortillas

INGREDIENTS

DRY INGREDIENTS

- ½ cup almond flour (50 g)
- ¼ cup coconut flour (30 g)
- ½ tsp. baking soda (2.5 g)
- ½ tsp. sea salt (2.5 g)
- 1 Tbsp. organic psyllium husk powder (12 g)
- 1 Tbsp. organic ground golden flaxseed (10 g)

WET INGREDIENTS

- 2 Tbsp. coconut oil (30 ml)
- 2 Tbsp. egg whites (60 g)
- ½ cup boiling water (120 ml)

DIRECTIONS

1. Preheat a tortilla press or a cast iron skillet over medium-high heat.

2. In a medium bowl, mix together the dry ingredients.

3. Add the coconut oil and mix with a fork or your hands to form a "shaggy" dough. Stir in the egg whites.

4. Pour in the boiling water, stirring quickly to incorporate. Dough will swell and become easy to work with.

5. Divide dough into 8 roughly one-ounce balls (28 g).

6. Place dough onto wax or parchment and flatten to a circle 4 inches (10 cm) in diameter.

7. Put flattened dough onto press or skillet. Cook 2-3 minutes. Flip once if using a skillet.

8. Best served immediately.

NUTRITION INFORMATION

86 calories, 7 g fat, 3 g saturated fat, 2 g monounsaturated fat, 1 g polyunsaturated fat, 0 mg cholesterol, 5 g carbohydrate, 1 g NET carbs, 0 g sugar alcohols, 1 g sugar, 3g fiber, 2 g protein, 67 mg potassium, 12 mg phosphorous, 230 mg sodium, 25 mg magnesium

MACRONUTRIENT RATIO

80% FAT ▪ 12% PROTEIN ▪ 8% CARBOHYDRATE

KETO ROSEMARY FOCACCIA

This keto-friendly flatbread is crispy on the bottom, fluffy on top... and a dead ringer for Italy's favorite bread. Enjoy this old-world favorite for sandwiches or as it is meant to be served — dipped into a high-quality olive oil!

YIELD: Two 8-inch Focaccias (16 slices)

INGREDIENTS

LEAVENING INGREDIENTS

- ½ cup filtered water (120 ml)
- 2 tsp. yeast (6 g)
- 2 tsp. maple syrup or honey (10 ml)*

WET INGREDIENTS

- 3 large pastured eggs (150 g)
- 6 Tbsp. extra virgin olive oil (84 g)
- ¼ cup organic yogurt, sour cream, coconut cream or *Dairy-Free Sour Cream* (page 110) (60 g)

- 1 Tbsp. organic apple cider vinegar (15 ml)

DRY INGREDIENTS

- 1½ cups almond flour (150 g)
- ⅔ cup golden flax meal (80 g)
- ½ tsp. garlic powder (2.5 g)
- 2 Tbsp. psyllium husk powder (18 g)
- 2 tsp. non-aluminum baking powder (10 g)

Ingredients continued...

- 1 tsp. sea salt (5 g)
- ¼ tsp. cream of tartar (0.75 g)
- 2 tsp. grass-fed beef gelatin (6 g)

EXTRAS

- 6 sprigs fresh rosemary
- ½ tsp flaky sea salt (like Maldon)

DIRECTIONS

1. Line two 8" round pans with unbleached parchment paper. Break rosemary sprigs into small clusters, removing the woody stems.

2. Add the yeast and sweetener* (maple syrup or honey) to a large bowl. Heat water to 105°F - 110°F (41°C - 43°C) and pour over yeast. Cover with a kitchen towel to bloom for 7 minutes. If yeast does not produce foam, start over.

3. Mix the dry ingredients in a small bowl.

4. In another bowl, whisk the eggs, vinegar, sour cream and olive oil.

5. Add the wet ingredients into the yeast mixture. Using a hand held mixer, beat to combine. Pour in the dry ingredients and beat on medium to fully combine.

6. Scrape batter into prepared pans. Wet your hands and smooth the batter. Use your fingers to make indentations. Put the rosemary sprigs in some of the holes. Drizzle with remaining olive oil.

7. Cover with a kitchen towel and place in a draft-free area to rise for 50 minutes. Your bread should rise to about 1 inch.

8. Preheat oven to 350°F (177°C). Sprinkle risen focaccia with flaky sea salt and transfer to the oven. Bake 25-30 minutes.

9. Cool focaccia in the pan on a wire rack, then transfer to a wire rack to cool completely.

***NOTE**: Sweetener is used to feed the yeast. Once the yeast blooms, no sweetener remains.

NUTRITION INFORMATION

156 calories, 14 g fat, 2 g saturated fat, 8 g monounsaturated fat, 3 g polyunsaturated fat, 40 mg cholesterol, 5 g carbohydrate, 2 g NET carbs, 0 g sugar alcohols, 0.5 g sugar, 4 g fiber, 5 g protein, 205 mg potassium, 145 mg phosphorous, 168 mg sodium, 49 mg magnesium

MACRONUTRIENT RATIO

83% FAT ■ 12% PROTEIN ■ 5% CARBOHYDRATE

QUICK KETO FOCACCIA

This fluffy, nut-free bread is a tasty option for those who can't have tree nuts. You can also make a standard loaf or typical round focaccia-style bread. For deliciously simple "white" bread, omit the herbs and garlic.

YIELD: 16 sheet-pan slices (with option for standard 9" x 5" (23 x 12 cm) loa

INGREDIENTS

DRY INGREDIENTS

- ¾ tsp. baking soda (4 g)
- ½ tsp. sea salt (2.5 g)
- 2 tsp. garlic powder (8 g)
- ½ Tbsp. dried organic herbs (basil, herbes de Provence or Tuscan) (2 g)

WET INGREDIENTS

- 5 pastured eggs, room temperature (250 g)
- ¼ cup coconut oil, melted (60 ml)
- One 7 oz. pack *Let's Do Organic Creamed Coconut* (200 g)*
- 5 oil-cured sun-dried tomatoes, patted dry and cut into strips

DIRECTIONS

1. Preheat oven to 300°F (149°C).

2. Grease a 13" x 9" (33 x 23 cm) sheet pan or line with parchment. Place creamed coconut – in its plastic packaging – in a bowl of warm water to soften.

3. In a high-powered blender, add the eggs, softened coconut cream and melted coconut oil. Blend on medium until smooth. Add the salt, baking soda and garlic powder. Blend again to combine. Stir in the herbs.

4. Pour batter onto the prepared sheet pan. (The batter will be the consistency of a thick pancake batter. Don't worry, it will firm up).

5. Scatter the sun-dried tomatoes over the top of the batter.

6. Transfer to oven and bake 20 minutes or until a toothpick comes out clean and bread is golden.

7. Cool on a wire rack. When completely cool, store in an airtight container.

STANDARD LOAF: To create a 9" x 5" (23 x 12 cm) loaf, pour into a prepared pan and bake until bread is firm to the touch and a toothpick comes out clean, about 50 minutes. **FOR WHITE BREAD**: Omit garlic powder, herbs and sun-dried tomatoes and bake in a standard loaf pan.

***NOTE**: Creamed coconut is unsweetened, dehydrated coconut, ground into a paste. It should contain no additives (not even water). If *Let's Do Organic* is unavailable or you have trouble finding "creamed coconut", look for coconut butter or coconut concentrate. Please note that "coconut cream" is the cream on top of a can of coconut milk – it is <u>NOT</u> the same as "creamed coconut".

NUTRITION INFORMATION

145 calories, 13 g fat, 11 g saturated fat, 2 g monounsaturated fat, 0.3 g polyunsaturated fat, 66 mg cholesterol, 4 g carbohydrate, 2 g NET carbs, 0 g sugar alcohols, 1 g sugar, 3 g fiber, 2 g protein, 26 mg potassium, 32 mg phosphorous, 226 mg sodium, 2 mg magnesium

MACRONUTRIENT RATIO

89% FAT ■ 6% PROTEIN ■ 5% CARBOHYDRATE

ZUCCHINI PANINI BREAD

This light and chewy batter bread is no-fuss to make (and a great way to sneak in a serving of veggies). Bake to golden, slice and enjoy right away. Or use a Panini press to create delicious Keto-friendly sandwiches.

YIELD: One 13" x 9" (33 x 23 cm) pan (6-12 slices depending on preferred s

INGREDIENTS

DRY INGREDIENTS

- 1¼ cup almond flour (120 g)
- 1 Tbsp. coconut flour (6 g)
- ½ Tbsp. grass-fed gelatin (4.5 g)
- ½ Tbsp. non-aluminum baking powder (7.5 g)
- ½ tsp. sea salt (2.5 g)

WET INGREDIENTS

- 1 cup organic zucchini, peeled and roughly chopped (130 g)
- 2 pastured eggs + 2 egg whites (160 g)
- ½ Tbsp. lemon juice (7.5 ml)

DIRECTIONS

1. Grease the bottom of a 13" x 9" (33 x 23 cm) sheet pan. Place a piece of parchment on bottom of the greased pan.

2. Preheat oven to 350°F (177°C).

3. In a high-powered blender, add the zucchini, eggs and lemon juice. Blend until smooth.

4. In a medium bowl, whisk the dry ingredients.

5. Pour the pureed zucchini mixture into the dry ingredients. Whisk well to combine.

6. Pour batter onto pan. Spread batter evenly in a thin layer.

7. Transfer to oven. Bake 25 minutes (rotate the pan after 12 minutes for more even browning).

8. Cool on a wire rack. Peel parchment off of the back and slice into squares.

9. Fill with meat and cheeses and grill on a cast-iron grill or in a Panini press.

10. Store cooled bread in an airtight container.

NUTRITION INFORMATION (PER 2" X 2" OR 5 X 5 CM SLICE)

77 calories, 6 g fat, 1 g saturated fat, 3 g monounsaturated fat, 1 g polyunsaturated fat, 35 mg cholesterol, 3 g carbohydrate, 2 g NET carbs, 0 g sugar alcohols, 1 g sugar, 2 g fiber, 4 g protein, 226 mg potassium, 80 mg phosphorous, 113 mg sodium, 34 mg magnesium

MACRONUTRIENT RATIO

68% FAT ■ 22% PROTEIN ■ 10% CARBOHYDRATE

Breakfast
Breads

ENGLISH MUFFINS

Perfect for making your favorite Eggs Benedict or donning a simple slather of butter, you'll love the chewy texture of these authentic English Muffins.

YIELD: 4 large English muffins

INGREDIENTS

DRY INGREDIENTS

- ½ cup coconut flour (50 g)
- 1 Tbsp. psyllium husk powder (12 g)
- ½ tsp. non-aluminum baking powder (2.5 g)
- ½ tsp. sea salt (2.5g)
- ¼ tsp. cream of tartar (1 g)

WET INGREDIENTS

- 4 pastured eggs (200 g)
- 1 Tbsp. avocado oil or extra virgin olive oil (15 ml)
- 4 Tbsp. filtered water (60 ml)

DIRECTIONS

1. Preheat oven to 350°F (177°C).

2. Prepare a USA Pans Mini Round Cake Pan by lightly greasing.

3. In a small bowl, whisk the dry ingredients.

4. In another small bowl, whisk the wet ingredients until combined.

5. Sift the dry ingredients into the wet. Mix well using a silicone spatula to form a smooth, thick batter.

6. Use a ladle to scoop batter. Pour the mixture evenly into greased circles.

7. Transfer to oven. Bake 15-18 minutes or until golden and a toothpick inserted into the center comes out clean.

8. Cool on a wire rack. When completely cooled, store in an airtight container in the refrigerator.

NUTRITION INFORMATION

141 calories, 9 g fat, 3 g saturated fat, 4 g monounsaturated fat, 1 g polyunsaturated fat, 212mg cholesterol, 7g carbohydrate, 2 g NET carbs, 0 g sugar alcohols, 1 g sugar, 4g fiber, 7 g protein, 156 mg potassium, 138 mg phosphorous, 351 mg sodium, 6 mg magnesium

MACRONUTRIENT RATIO

69% FAT ■ 23% PROTEIN ■ 8% CARBOHYDRATE

BETTER BAGELS

Our golden, chewy version of this breakfast favorite is the perfect vehicle for Paleo Cream "Cheese" (page 112) and smoked wild salmon.

YIELD: 4 bagels

INGREDIENTS

DRY INGREDIENTS

- 1 cup almond flour (105 g)
- 2 Tbsp. coconut flour, firmly packed (14 g)
- 1 Tbsp. ground golden flaxseed (7.5 g)
- ½ Tbsp. arrowroot powder (4 g)
- ½ tsp. baking soda (2.5 g)
- ¼ tsp. sea salt (1.3 g)
- Sesame seeds, poppy seeds, *Maldon* sea salt, dried onion flakes (for topping)

WET INGREDIENTS

- 2 pastured eggs (100 g)
- 2 Tbsp. organic apple cider vinegar (30 ml)

DIRECTIONS

1. Preheat oven to 350°F (177°C).

2. Lightly grease a *USA Pans Donut Pan*.

3. In a small bowl, whisk together the dry ingredients.

4. In another small bowl, whisk the wet ingredients until combined.

5. Add dry ingredients to wet and mix using a silicone spatula to form a thick batter.

6. Use a ladle to transfer about ¼ cup (60 ml) of batter into each greased circle.

7. Sprinkle with toppings of choice.

8. Transfer to oven. Bake 18-20 minutes or until golden and a toothpick inserted into the center comes out clean.

9. Cool on a wire rack. Serve freshly baked or toasted with *Paleo Cream "Cheese"* (page 112) or your toppings of choice

10. Store cooled bagels in an airtight container in the refrigerator.

NUTRITION INFORMATION

194 calories, 15 g fat, 2 g saturated fat, 8 g monounsaturated fat, 4 g polyunsaturated fat, 106 mg cholesterol, 8 g carbohydrate, 4 g NET carbs, 0 g sugar alcohols, 1 g sugar, 4 g fiber, 9 g protein, 239 mg potassium, 60 mg phosphorous, 343 mg sodium, 81 mg magnesium

MACRONUTRIENT RATIO

73% FAT ■ 19% PROTEIN ■ 8% CARBOHYDRATE

SUPERFAT NY BAGELS

These ketogenic bagels are full of healthy fats, very low in carbs and take just 15 minutes (active time) to make. And once you have a taste, you'll never crave the grain-filled, carb-laden variety again!

YIELD: 6 bagels

INGREDIENTS

- 8 ounces organic pre-shredded mozzarella cheese (227 g)
- 2 ounces organic cream cheese (56 g)
- 1½ cups almond flour (150 g)
- 3 tsp. non-aluminum baking powder (15 g)
- 2 large pastured eggs (100 g)
- Sesame seeds, poppy seeds, *Maldon* sea salt, dried onion flakes (for topping)

DIRECTIONS

1. Preheat oven to 400°F (204°C).

2. Line a baking sheet with parchment paper or lightly grease a bagel/donut pan.

3. Place the cheeses in a microwaveable container. Microwave on high for 2 minutes, stirring after 1 minute, to melt the cheese. You may also melt the cheese in a double boiler over the stovetop. Stir until well incorporated.

4. Whisk the almond flour with baking powder.

5. Add the dry ingredients and eggs to the cheese mixture. Stir to combine. Using your hands, knead the dough to a uniform consistency. It may seem like it will not combine. Keep kneading. If needed, microwave the mixture in 20 second bursts to soften.

6. Divide dough into 6 pieces. Roll each into a log and pinch the ends together to make a circle.

7. Place bagels on a baking sheet or in a prepared donut pan. For a shiny crust, brush with an egg wash. Sprinkle with toppings, if using.

8. Transfer to preheated oven. Bake 11-14 minutes until golden and firm.

9. Store cooled bagels in an airtight container in the refrigerator.

NUTRITION INFORMATION

332 calories, 27 g fat, 9 g saturated fat, 13 g monounsaturated fat, 4 g polyunsaturated fat, 110 mg cholesterol, 8 g carbohydrate, 5 g NET carbs, 0 g sugar alcohols, 2 g sugar, 3 g fiber, 17 g protein, 511 mg potassium, 481 mg phosphorous, 288 mg sodium, 86 mg magnesium

MACRONUTRIENT RATIO

74% FAT ■ 21% PROTEIN ■ 6% CARBOHYDRATE

SOUTHERN-STYLE BISCUITS

With a classic golden-crisp crust and a dense interior, these low-carb biscuits are the perfect accompaniment for sausage gravy or for topping a Keto pot pie.

YIELD: 6 biscuits

INGREDIENTS

DRY INGREDIENTS

- ⅔ cup coconut flour (65 g)
- ¼ cup almond flour (25 g)
- 2 Tbsp. arrowroot powder (18 g)
- 1 tsp. non-aluminum baking powder (5 g)
- ¼ tsp. sea salt (1.3 g)

WET INGREDIENTS

- 2 Tbsp. cold pastured butter or *Nutiva Superfood Shortening* or virgin coconut oil (solid) (30 g)
- 6 egg whites (180 g)

DIRECTIONS

1. Preheat oven to 400°F (204°C).

2. Lightly grease a muffin tin or a baking sheet.

3. In a medium bowl, whisk the dry ingredients.

4. Add the solid butter, shortening or coconut oil to the dry ingredients.

5. Use a pastry blender or two knives, cut the oil or butter into the flour until the entire mixture is crumbly. Place the flour mixture in the refrigerator.

6. In a Magic Bullet or blender, add the egg whites. Blend until very frothy.

7. Pour the egg whites into the flour mixture and fold in gently. The dough will expand and become sturdy.

8. 8Use a scoop or pick up dough by ¼ cupful (60 ml) and place onto prepared pan. Shape as desired.

9. Transfer to oven. Bake 17-20 minutes or until golden.

10. Cool on a wire rack.

11. Store in an airtight container in the refrigerator. Toast to re-crisp before eating.

NUTRITION INFORMATION

122 calories, 7 g fat, 4 g saturated fat, 2 g monounsaturated fat, 1 g polyunsaturated fat, 10 mg cholesterol, 10 g carbohydrate, 5 g NET carbs, 0 g sugar alcohols, 1 g sugar, 4g fiber, 6 g protein, 170 mg potassium, 63 mg phosphorous, 190 mg sodium, 16 mg magnesium

MACRONUTRIENT RATIO

59% FAT ■ 21% PROTEIN ■ 19% CARBOHYDRATE

KETO DROP BISCUITS

Just like the classic, these drop biscuits have crisp peaks on the outside with fluffy, tender centers. Feel free to throw in your favorite shredded cheese, cracked black pepper or fresh herbs. And for the most authentic results, bake in a cast iron pan.

YIELD: 6 biscuits

INGREDIENTS

- ⅔ cup almond flour (67 g)
- ½ cup coconut flour (45 g)
- 2 Tbsp. ground golden flaxseeds (14 g)
- 1 tsp. non-aluminum baking powder (5 g)
- 2 Tbsp. cold grass-fed butter or palm shortening (28 g)
- 5 large organic egg whites (165 g)

DIRECTIONS

1. Place butter in the freezer to chill, about 15 minutes.

2. In a medium bowl, whisk the almond flour, coconut flour, flax and baking powder.

3. Chop chilled butter into small pieces. Add cold butter to flour ingredients. Mix with hands or pastry blender to the consistency of coarse sand. Transfer mixture to the freezer to chill.

4. Preheat oven to 425°F (218°C).

5. Prepare a cast iron griddle (preferred) or cookie sheet.

6. Whip egg whites to stiff peaks. Fold whipped whites into flour mixture to form a thick batter. Scoop by 2 Tbsp. onto prepared pan, shaping gently.

7. Bake for 16-18 minutes until golden.

8. Cool on a wire rack.

9. Store in an airtight container in the refrigerator. Toast to re-crisp before eating.

NUTRITION INFORMATION

104 calories, 9 g fat, 4 g saturated fat, 3 g monounsaturated fat, 1 g polyunsaturated fat, 0 mg cholesterol, 3 g carbohydrate, 1 g NET carbs, 0 g sugar alcohols, 1 g sugar, 2 g fiber, 4 g protein, 161 mg potassium, 88 mg phosphorous, 46 mg sodium, 30 mg magnesium

MACRONUTRIENT RATIO

80% FAT ■ 15% PROTEIN ■ 5% CARBOHYDRATE

Rolls &
Buns

PALEO FRIENDLY · **3 NET CARBS** · **DAIRY FREE**

BETTER BURGER BUNS & SUB ROLLS

If you're tired of eating juicy, grass-fed burgers in a wilting lettuce wrap, these soft and chewy buns are the solution! They are a snap to make and keep well in the refrigerator.

YIELD: 4 large burger buns or 4 small sub rolls

INGREDIENTS

DRY INGREDIENTS

- 1¼ cups almond flour (115 g)
- 1 Tbsp. organic psyllium husk powder (12 g)
- 1 tsp. baking soda (5 g)
- ½ tsp. sea salt (2.5 g)

WET INGREDIENTS

- 3 egg whites (90 g)
- 1 tsp. organic apple cider vinegar (5 ml)
- ⅔ cup boiling water (160 ml)

DIRECTIONS

1. Preheat oven to 350°F (177°C). Prepare a baking sheet with parchment.

2. In a medium bowl, combine the dry ingredients.

3. In a small bowl whisk the egg whites and apple cider vinegar.

4. Add wet ingredients to dry and mix using a handheld mixer or silicone spatula to form a thick batter.

5. Pour in hot water and quickly mix to incorporate. The dough will become more sticky and pliable, similar to thick oatmeal.

6. Divide into four equally-sized balls and place on prepared sheet. Flatten to roughly 1-inch (2.5 cm) thickness. The buns should rise to about 2½ inches (6 cm) in height.

7. Sprinkle with flaky sea salt or sesame seeds, if desired.

8. Transfer to oven and bake 40-50 minutes.

9. Cool on a wire rack and store cooled buns and sub rolls in an airtight container.

NUTRITION INFORMATION

191 calories, 15 g fat, 1 g saturated fat, 9 g monounsaturated fat, 3 g polyunsaturated fat, 0 mg cholesterol, 9 g carbohydrate, 3 g NET carbs, 0 g sugar alcohols, 1 g sugar, 5 g fiber, 9 g protein, 279 mg potassium, 4 mg phosphorous, 648 mg sodium, 92 mg magnesium

MACRONUTRIENT RATIO

73% FAT ■ 20% PROTEIN ■ 7% CARBOHYDRATE

KETO BURGER BUNS

This sturdy bun will hold up to even the juiciest burger and highest pile of toppings. Better yet, the authentic texture and flavor will please even the most critical burger lovers!

YIELD: 8 burger buns

INGREDIENTS

LEAVENING INGREDIENTS

- ½ cup filtered water (120 ml)
- 2 tsp. yeast (6 g)
- 2 tsp. maple syrup or honey (10 ml)*

WET INGREDIENTS

- 3 large pastured eggs (150 g)
- ¼ cup grass-fed butter or coconut oil, melted (56 g)
- ¼ cup organic yogurt, sour cream, *Dairy Free Sour Cream* (page 110) or coconut cream (60 g)
- 1 Tbsp. organic apple cider vinegar (15 ml)

Ingredients continued...

KETO *Breads*

DRY INGREDIENTS

- 1½ cups almond flour (150 g)
- ⅔ cup golden flax meal (80 g)
- 2 Tbsp. psyllium husk powder (18 g)
- 2 tsp. non-aluminum baking powder (10 g)

- 1 tsp. sea salt (5 g)
- ¼ tsp. cream of tartar (0.75 g)
- 2 tsp. grass-fed beef gelatin (6 g)
- 2 tsp. sesame seeds for topping (5 g)

DIRECTIONS

1. Grease a hamburger pan (we like *USA Pans Mini Round Cake Pans*).
2. Add the yeast and 2 tsp. sweetener* (maple syrup or honey) to a large bowl. Heat water to 105°F – 110°F (41°C - 43°C) and pour over yeast. Cover with a kitchen towel to bloom for 7 minutes.
3. In a small bowl, mix the almond flour, flaxseed powder, psyllium husk powder, baking powder, sea salt, cream of tartar and gelatin.
4. In another bowl, whisk the eggs, vinegar, sour cream and melted butter.
5. Add the wet ingredients into the yeast mixture. Using a hand held mixer, beat to combine.
6. Pour in the dry ingredients and beat on medium speed to fully combine.
7. Divide batter among wells of pan. For a shiny, golden crust, gently brush with egg wash. Sprinkle with sesame seeds.
8. Cover with a kitchen towel and place in a draft-free area to rise for 50 minutes. Your rolls will rise roughly 1 inch.
9. While your dough is rising, preheat oven to 350°F (177°C).
10. Transfer risen dough to oven and bake 25-30 minutes to golden brown.
11. Cool in the pan on a wire rack for 30 minutes. Then remove from pan and cool completely on wire rack before slicing.

*NOTE: Sweetener is used to feed the yeast. Once yeast blooms, no sweetener remains.

NUTRITION INFORMATION

271 calories, 23 g fat, 6 g saturated fat, 10 g monounsaturated fat, 6 g polyunsaturated fat, 0 mg cholesterol, 10 g carbohydrate, 4 g NET carbs, 0 g sugar alcohols, 1 g sugar, 7 g fiber, 9 g protein, 408 mg potassium, 294 mg phosphorous, 377 mg sodium, 99 mg magnesium

MACRONUTRIENT RATIO

80% FAT ■ 15% PROTEIN ■ 6% CARBOHYDRATE

HERBED DINNER ROLLS

Not quite a biscuit and not quite a bun, these light-textured rolls make a wonderful, buttery, golden accompaniment to traditional American meals.

YIELD: 12 rolls

INGREDIENTS

DRY INGREDIENTS

- ¾ cup coconut flour (80 g)
- 2 tsp. cream of tartar (6 g)
- 1 tsp. baking soda (5 g)
- ½ tsp. sea salt (2.5 g)

WET INGREDIENTS

- ½ cup pastured butter, cold or *Superfood Shortening* (114 g)
- ¼ cup chopped fresh parsley (60 ml)
- ¼ cup chopped fresh chives (60 ml)
- 5 pastured eggs (250 g)
- ½ cup light coconut milk (120 ml) OR ¼ cup full fat coconut milk (60 ml) + ¼ cup water (60 ml)

DIRECTIONS

1. Preheat oven to 450°F (232°C). Add liners or lightly grease a muffin tin.

2. In a medium bowl, whisk the dry ingredients.

3. Using a pastry blender or two knives, cut in the butter or shortening until crumbly.

4. In a separate bowl, whisk the eggs and coconut milk. Pour wet ingredients over dry and mix with a fork to combine. The mixture will be soupy with lumps. Let stand for 5 minutes to thicken.

5. Scoop batter into the muffin tin. Batter should fill cups halfway.

6. Transfer to oven and bake 11-13 minutes or until golden and a toothpick inserted into the center comes out clean.

7. Cool on a wire rack. Store in an airtight container in the refrigerator.

NUTRITION INFORMATION

150 calories, 15g fat, 10 g saturated fat, 3 g monounsaturated fat, 1 g polyunsaturated fat, 108 mg cholesterol, 2 g carbohydrate, 1 g NET carbs, 0 g sugar alcohols, 1 g sugar, 1 g fiber, 3 g protein, 139 mg potassium, 58 mg phosphorous, 299 mg sodium, 12 mg magnesium

MACRONUTRIENT RATIO

88% FAT ■ 9% PROTEIN ■ 3% CARBOHYDRATE

"SECRET INGREDIENT" DINNER ROLLS

Crispy on the outside, chewy on the inside, these tender rolls are perfect for slathering with butter, sopping up sauces or filling with your favorite meats.

YIELD: 12 rolls

INGREDIENTS

DRY INGREDIENTS

- 2 Tbsp. organic psyllium husk powder (24 g)
- ½ cup coconut flour (50 g)
- ½ tsp. sea salt (2.5 g)
- 3 tsp. non-aluminum baking powder (15 g)
- 3 tsp. organic dried basil (or dried herb or choice)

WET INGREDIENTS

- 4 large pastured eggs (200 g)
- 2 Tbsp. avocado oil, or melted coconut oil (30 ml)
- 2 Tbsp. organic apple cider vinegar (30 ml)
- 1 medium zucchini*, finely grated (196 g)
- ¼ cup filtered water (60 ml)

DIRECTIONS

1. Preheat your oven to 350°F (177°C). Grease a sheet pan.

2. In a large bowl, combine the dry ingredients.

3. In a medium bowl, stir together the wet ingredients.

4. Add dry ingredients to wet and mix with an electric mixer on medium speed to fully combine.

5. Grease hands and scoop dough out by golfball-sized mounds. Roll gently to desired shape and place on baking sheet.

6. Brush with avocado oil and transfer to oven. Bake for 1 hour to golden brown.

7. Cool on a wire rack. Store in an airtight container in the refrigerator.

*And the "secret ingredient" is zucchini – a delicious way to sneak in a serving of veggies.

NUTRITION INFORMATION

74 calories, 5g fat, 1 g saturated fat, 2 g monounsaturated fat, 1 g polyunsaturated fat, 71 mg cholesterol, 5 g carbohydrate, 2 g NET carbs, 0 g sugar alcohols, 1 g sugar, 3 g fiber, 3 g protein, 197 mg potassium,124 mg phosphorous, 133 mg sodium, 6 mg magnesium

MACRONUTRIENT RATIO

67% FAT ▪ 19% PROTEIN ▪ 14% CARBOHYDRATE

SUPERFAT DINNER ROLLS

With a crispy "hard roll" exterior and pillow-soft crumb, these golden rolls make the perfect accompaniment to your favorite keto soups and stews.

YIELD: 8 rolls

INGREDIENTS

- 8 ounces organic pre-shredded mozzarella cheese (227 g)
- 1½ cups almond flour (150 g)
- 2 ounces organic cream cheese (56 g)
- 3 tsp. non-aluminum baking powder (15 g)
- 2 large pastured eggs (100 g)
- 1 large egg white (30 g)
- 2 tsp. sesame seeds or poppy seeds (optional)

DIRECTIONS

1. Preheat oven to 400°F (204°C). Line a baking sheet with unbleached parchment paper.

2. Place the cheeses in a microwaveable container. Microwave on high for 2 minutes, stirring after 1 minute, to melt the cheese. You may also melt the cheese in a double boiler over the stovetop. Stir until well incorporated.

3. Whisk the almond flour with baking powder.

4. Add the dry ingredients and whole eggs to the cheese mixture and stir to combine. Use your hands to knead the dough to a uniform consistency. It may seem like it will not combine. Keep kneading. If needed, microwave in 20 second bursts to soften the mixture.

5. Divide dough into 8 pieces. Roll each into a ball and place on baking sheet. Brush with egg white and sprinkle with seeds, if using.

6. Transfer to preheated oven and bake 11-14 minutes until golden and firm.

7. Cool on a wire rack. Store in an airtight container in the refrigerator.

NUTRITION INFORMATION

255 calories, 21g fat, 6 g saturated fat, 10 g monounsaturated fat, 3 g polyunsaturated fat, 83 mg cholesterol, 7 g carbohydrate, 4 g NET carbs, 0 g sugar alcohols, 1 g sugar, 3 g fiber, 13 g protein, 394 mg potassium, 366 mg phosphorous, 223 mg sodium, 67 mg magnesium

MACRONUTRIENT RATIO

73% FAT ■ 21% PROTEIN ■ 6% CARBOHYDRATE

CHEDDAR SLIDER BUNS

Reinvent last night's leftover meat with these fast-and-easy buns. Feel free to swap out cheddar for your cheese of choice. Try asiago with balsamic beef for a Mediterranean twist or pulled pork with Pepper Jack for Southern charm.

YIELD: 8 buns (4 servings)

INGREDIENTS

- 3 ounces organic pre-shredded mozzarella cheese (85 g)
- 2 ounces organic cream cheese (56 g)
- 1 large pastured egg (50 g)
- ⅓ cup almond flour (33 g)
- 2 tsp. non-aluminum baking powder (10 g)
- 1 ounce organic cheddar cheese, shredded (28 g)

DIRECTIONS

1. Grease a baking sheet or line with unbleached parchment paper.

2. In a small glass bowl, add the mozzarella and cream cheese. Microwave on high for 30 seconds. Stir and return to microwave in 30-second increments, until melted completely.

3. In a small bowl, whisk the almond flour, egg and baking powder. Stir almond flour mixture into the melted cheese mixture to fully combine. Stir in shredded cheddar.

4. Place dough on plastic wrap and cover. Transfer to refrigerator for 20 minutes. Preheat oven to 425°F (218°C).

5. Cut the dough ball into 4 pieces, and then halve those pieces. Roll into 8 small balls. Place balls 2" apart on prepared baking sheet.

6. Transfer to oven and bake 10-12 minutes or until golden.

7. Cool on a wire rack. Store in an airtight container in the refrigerator.

NUTRITION INFORMATION

214 calories, 18g fat, 8 g saturated fat, 7 g monounsaturated fat, 2 g polyunsaturated fat, 92 mg cholesterol, 4 g carbohydrate, 3 g NET carbs, 0 g sugar alcohols, 1 g sugar, 1 g fiber, 11 g protein, 374 mg potassium, 365 mg phosphorous, 236 mg sodium, 34 mg magnesium

MACRONUTRIENT RATIO

74% FAT ■ 20% PROTEIN ■ 6% CARBOHYDRATE

Crackers, Croutons & Crusts

KETO CROUTONS & BREADCRUMBS

What's a Caesar salad... without croutons? Boasting near identical taste and texture as the grain-and-carb filled original, these croutons can be whipped up quickly and frozen – or pulsed in the blender to make keto-friendly breadcrumbs.

YIELD: 4 cups croutons / 3¼ cups breadcrumbs (16 servings)

INGREDIENTS

DRY INGREDIENTS

- ¾ tsp. baking soda (4 g)
- ½ tsp. sea salt (2.5 g)
- ½ tsp. garlic powder (2 g)

WET INGREDIENTS

- 5 pastured eggs, room temperature (250 g)
- ¼ cup coconut oil, melted (60 ml)
- One 7 oz. pack *Let's Do Organic Creamed Coconut* (200 g)*

DIRECTIONS

1. Preheat oven to 300°F (149°C).

2. Grease a 13" x 9" (33 x 23 cm) sheet pan or line with parchment. Place creamed coconut – in its plastic packaging – in a bowl of warm water to soften.

3. In a high-powered blender, add the eggs, softened coconut cream and melted coconut oil. Blend on medium until smooth. Add the salt, baking soda and garlic powder. Blend to combine.

4. Pour the batter onto the prepared sheet pan. The batter will be the consistency of a thick pancake batter. Don't be alarmed. It will firm up.

5. Transfer to oven and bake 40 minutes until golden brown and firm.

6. Cool and then slice bread into dice-sized cubes. Place bread cubes back onto a baking sheet. Drizzle with olive oil and garlic powder (if desired) and toast on "medium" in a toaster oven for 6 minutes to crisp.

7. Store in an airtight container or freeze in a zip-top freezer bag.

8. For breadcrumbs, add croutons to a blender or food processor and pulse. Use in meatballs and meatloaf, or for breading meats.

*NOTE: Creamed coconut is unsweetened, dehydrated coconut, ground into a paste. It should contain no additives (not even water). If *Let's Do Organic* is unavailable or you have trouble finding "creamed coconut", look for coconut butter or coconut concentrate. Please note that "coconut cream" is the cream on top of a can of coconut milk – it is <u>NOT</u> the same as "creamed coconut".

NUTRITION INFORMATION

137 calories, 13 g fat, 11 g saturated fat, 2 g monounsaturated fat, 0.3 g polyunsaturated fat, 66 mg cholesterol, 3 g carbohydrate, 1 g NET carbs, 0 g sugar alcohols, 1 g sugar, 2 g fiber, 2 g protein, 25 mg potassium, 31 mg phosphorous, 158 mg sodium, 2 mg magnesium

MACRONUTRIENT RATIO

90% FAT ■ 6% PROTEIN ■ 4% CARBOHYDRATE

HERBED CHEDDAR CRACKERS

These crisp and cheesy herbed crackers are quick to prepare. But they disappear fast, so make a double batch!

YIELD: 16 crackers

INGREDIENTS

- ½ cup almond flour (50 g)
- ¼ cup coconut flour (25 g)
- 2 Tbsp. grass-fed butter (30 g)
- 2 ounces organic cheddar cheese, grated (56 g)
- 1 tsp. dried rosemary (1 g)
- Flaky salt for sprinkling (optional)

DIRECTIONS

1. Preheat oven to 350°F (177°C). Grease a cookie sheet or line with parchment paper.

2. In a medium bowl, add almond flour, coconut flour and butter.

3. Using a pastry blender or fork, mix until pea-sized pieces form.

4. Add cheese and mix dough to a uniform consistency. Stir in rosemary.

5. Form a log and chill 15-20 minutes. Slice into rounds ¼-inch thick. You may also roll the dough to ¼ inch thickness between two pieces of parchment paper and then use a cookie cutter.

6. Place rounds on a greased cookie sheet. Sprinkle with flaky sea salt.

7. Bake for 8-10 minutes until golden. Cool on a wire rack.

8. Store in an airtight container in the refrigerator.

NUTRITION INFORMATION

57 calories, 5 g fat, 3 g saturated fat, 2 g monounsaturated fat, 0.5 g polyunsaturated fat, 7 mg cholesterol, 1 g carbohydrate, 0.5 g NET carbs, 0 g sugar alcohols, 0.3 g sugar, 1 g fiber, 2 g protein, 36 mg potassium, 38 mg phosphorous, 33 mg sodium, 12 mg magnesium

MACRONUTRIENT RATIO

85% FAT ■ 12% PROTEIN ■ 3% CARBOHYDRATE

SESAME-DIJON CRACKERS

These crackers are sturdy and crisp — and pair perfectly with smoked wild salmon, olive tapenade, sardines and your favorite grass-fed cheeses. Feel free to swap the tahini for almond butter or sunflower seed butter.

YIELD: 16 crackers (1 cracker per serving)

INGREDIENTS

- 3 Tbsp. tahini paste (48 g)
- 1 pastured egg (50 g)
- 2 tsp. spicy brown mustard (10 ml)
- 2½ Tbsp. coconut flour, packed (22 g)
- 2 Tbsp. sesame seeds (16 g)
- ¼ tsp. fine sea salt (1.7 g)

DIRECTIONS

1. Preheat the oven to 325°F (163°C). Line a baking sheet with parchment paper.

2. In a medium bowl, whisk the egg, tahini and mustard with a fork until smooth. Add the coconut flour, salt and sesame seeds. Stir until a thick dough forms.

3. Place the dough on a piece of parchment and roll to ⅛ inch thick rectangle. Use a sharp knife to score the dough into 16 crackers.

4. Place the parchment with the dough onto a cookie sheet and transfer to the preheated oven. Bake for 15 minutes. Remove from oven and Cool for 15 minutes.

5. Turn oven down to 300°F (149°C) and return crackers to oven for another 10-12 minutes to crisp.

6. Cool before breaking apart. Store in an airtight container. Reheat in 300F oven to re-crisp, if necessary.

NUTRITION INFORMATION

34 calories, 3g fat, 1 g saturated fat, 1 g monounsaturated fat, 1 g polyunsaturated fat, 13 mg cholesterol, 1 g carbohydrate, 1 g NET carbs, 0 g sugar alcohols, 0.1 g sugar, 0. 4 g fiber, 1 g protein, 28mg potassium, 38 mg phosphorous, 49 mg sodium, 8 mg magnesium

MACRONUTRIENT RATIO

78% FAT ■ 14% PROTEIN ■ 8% CARBOHYDRATE

NO-RITOS NACHO CHIPS

When celery sticks and carrots just won't do for dipping into your famous guacamole or melted cheese sauce, these crispy chips will fit the bill!

YIELD: 36 chips (6 servings of 6 chips)

INGREDIENTS

DRY INGREDIENTS

- ¾ cup almond flour (80 g)
- ¼ cup coconut flour, firmly packed (25 g)
- 1 Tbsp. pumpkin seeds, finely ground (15 g)
- 1 Tbsp. chia seeds, finely ground (12 g)
- ½ tsp. sea salt (3.35 g)
- 2 tsp. chili powder (4 g)
- ½ tsp. cumin (1 g)
- ½ tsp. paprika or smoked paprika (1 g)
- ½ tsp. garlic powder (2.5 g)

Ingredients continued...

KETO *Breads*

WET INGREDIENTS

- 1 pastured egg (50 g)
- ¼ cup grass-fed butter or virgin coconut oil, melted (2 oz)

DIRECTIONS

1. Preheat oven to 350°F (177°C).

2. In a small bowl, combine the dry ingredients.

3. In a medium bowl, combine the wet ingredients, whisking well.

4. Add dry ingredients to wet and mix well to form a dough.

5. Place the dough ball on a piece of parchment paper. Top with another piece of parchment.

6. Roll the dough between the two papers into a rectangle with ⅛-inch thickness. Remove the top layer of parchment.

7. Trim the edges of the dough to get nice straight edges. Then slice the dough into triangles.

8. Place parchment with sliced dough on a cookie sheet. Transfer to oven and bake 8-10 minutes, watching to ensure they don't burn. Turn the oven off and allow chips to crisp another 10 minutes.

9. Store cooled chips in an airtight container.

NUTRITION INFORMATION

207 calories, 18g fat, 10 g saturated fat, 5 g monounsaturated fat, 3 g polyunsaturated fat, 35 mg cholesterol, 7 g carbohydrate, 3 g NET carbs, 0 g sugar alcohols, 1 g sugar, 4 g fiber, 5 g protein, 188 mg potassium, 48 mg phosphorous, 29 mg sodium, 52 mg magnesium

MACRONUTRIENT RATIO

83% FAT ■ 11% PROTEIN ■ 6% CARBOHYDRATE

KETO YEASTED PIZZA CRUST

Move over floppy cauliflower pizza crust! This risen NY-style crust is crisp and sturdy and makes the perfect vehicle for all your favorite toppings.

YIELD: One-10" pizza crust (6 servings)

INGREDIENTS

LEAVENING INGREDIENT

- ⅓ cup filtered water (80 ml)
- 2 tsp. yeast (6 g)
- 2 tsp. maple syrup or honey (10 ml)*

WET INGREDIENTS

- 2 large pastured eggs (100 g)
- 1 Tbsp. extra virgin olive (14 g)
- 2 tsp. organic apple cider vinegar (10 ml)

DRY INGREDIENTS

- 1 cup almond flour (100 g)
- ⅓ cup golden flax meal (37 g)
- 3 Tbsp. psyllium husk powder (27 g)
- 1½ tsp. non-aluminum baking powder (5 g)
- ½ tsp. sea salt (2.5 g)
- 1 tsp. grass-fed beef gelatin (3 g)

DIRECTIONS

1. Prepare a pizza stone or grease a baking sheet and line with parchment paper.

2. Add the yeast and 2 tsp. sweetener* to a large bowl. Heat water to 105°F - 110°F (41°C - 43°C) and pour over yeast. Cover with a kitchen towel to bloom for 7 minutes.

3. Meanwhile, mix the almond flour, flaxseed powder, psyllium husk powder, baking powder, sea salt, and gelatin in a small bowl.

4. In another bowl, whisk the eggs, vinegar, and oil.

5. Add the wet ingredients into the yeast mixture. Using a hand held mixer, beat to combine.

6. Pour in the dry ingredients and beat on medium speed to fully combine.

7. Scrape batter onto prepared pizza pan, and oil your hands. Gently shape dough with your fingers.

8. Cover with a kitchen towel (not touching the crust) and place in a draft-free area to rise for 50 minutes. Crust should rise from ½ to 1 inch.

9. Preheat oven to 350°F (177°C).

10. Transfer pizza to oven and bake 10-14 minutes. Add toppings and return to oven to melt cheese.

*NOTE: Sweetener is used to feed the yeast. Once yeast blooms, no sweetener remains.

NUTRITION INFORMATION

181 calories, 14 g fat, 2 g saturated fat, 7 g monounsaturated fat, 4 g polyunsaturated fat, 70 mg cholesterol, 10 g carbohydrate, 3 g NET carbs, 0 g sugar alcohols, 1 g sugar, 7 g fiber, 7 g protein, 282 mg potassium, 201 mg phosphorous, 232 mg sodium, 67 mg magnesium

MACRONUTRIENT RATIO

77% FAT ■ 17% PROTEIN ■ 6% CARBOHYDRATE

SUPERFAT PIZZA CRUST

This crisp-and-chewy crust is about as close as it gets in the grain-free world to the stretchy, gluten-filled original. If you can't have nuts, feel free to sub one-quarter cup of coconut flour for the almond flour in this recipe.

YIELD: One-10" pizza crust (6 servings)

INGREDIENTS

- 6 ounces organic pre-shredded mozzarella cheese (168 g)
- ¾ cup almond flour (75 g)
- 1 ounce organic cream cheese (28 g)
- 1 large pastured egg (50 g)
- 1 tsp Italian herbs (optional) (2 g)
- ½ tsp. garlic powder (optional) (2 g)

Ingredients continued...

DIRECTIONS

1. Preheat oven to 425°F (218°C). Prepare a pizza stone or grease a baking sheet and line with parchment paper.

2. Place mozzarella, cream cheese and almond flour in a microwaveable container. Microwave on high for 1 minute. Stir and microwave another 30 seconds.

3. Add the egg, garlic and herbs and knead the dough to a uniform consistency.

4. Place the dough between two pieces of parchment paper and roll out to a 10" circle.

5. Remove top sheet of parchment and place pizza on stone. Use a fork to poke holes in the pizza crust. Bake 11-14 minutes until crisp and golden.

6. Add toppings and return to oven to melt the cheese, about 5 minutes.

NUTRITION INFORMATION

193 calories, 16g fat, 5 g saturated fat, 7 g monounsaturated fat, 2 g polyunsaturated fat, 63 mg cholesterol, 4 g carbohydrate, 2 g NET carbs, 0 g sugar alcohols, 1 g sugar, 2 g fiber, 11 g protein, 137 mg potassium,188 mg phosphorous, 201 mg sodium, 44 mg magnesium

MACRONUTRIENT RATIO

74% FAT ■ 22% PROTEIN ■ 4% CARBOHYDRATE

Healthy Substitutions

HOMEMADE GRAIN-FREE BAKING POWDER

Most commercial baking powder contains both cornstarch and aluminum. The good news is you can easily make your own baking powder with just two simple ingredients.

YIELD: 36 tsp (160 g)

INGREDIENTS

- ¼ cup baking soda (60 g)
- ½ cup cream of tartar (100 g)

Ingredients continued...

DIRECTIONS

1. Mix the baking soda and cream of tartar in small jar.

2. Secure the lid and shake until well combined.

3. Store in a cool, dry place.

4. Use in any recipe that calls for baking powder.

DAIRY-FREE SOUR CREAM

If you avoid dairy, this recipe is a delicious stand-in for sour cream. It also lends moisture and tenderness to baked goods and is perfect with enchiladas or tacos, using No Gordita Tortillas (page 58).

YIELD: 2 cups (480 ml)

INGREDIENTS

- 2 cups organic coconut milk, chilled (480 ml)
- 1 tsp. (4 g) probiotic powder with nothing else added (like *iFlora Multi-Probiotic*)
- 1 pinch sea salt

Ingredients continued...

KETO *Breads*

DIRECTIONS

1. Place coconut milk in the refrigerator overnight. Open the containers and scoop the thick cream at the top into a small saucepan. Reserve the remaining water for smoothies or sauces.

2. Heat the coconut cream over the lowest heat to roughly 100°F (38°C). This will encourage probiotic cultures to multiply. Remove from the stove and whisk in probiotic powder.

3. Pour mixture into a quart jar. Cover with cheesecloth or a clean towel. Secure with a rubber band.

4. Let the jar sit for 24 – 48 hours on your kitchen counter. Then stir in a pinch or two of sea salt. Cover with a lid and place in the refrigerator to solidify.

NUTRITION INFORMATION

56 calories, 6 g fat, 5 g saturated fat, 1 g monounsaturated fat, 0 g polyunsaturated fat, 0 mg cholesterol, 1 g carbohydrate, 0.8 g NET carbs, 0 g sugar alcohols, 0 g sugar, 0 g fiber, 1 g protein, 62 mg potassium, 27 mg phosphorous, 8 mg sodium, 13 mg magnesium

MACRONUTRIENT RATIO

91% FAT ■ 4% PROTEIN ■ 5% CARBOHYDRATE

PALEO CREAM "CHEESE"

This simple recipe provides a deliciously-tangy, dairy-free alternative.
Use in recipes that call for cream cheese or enjoy a "schmear" atop
Better Bagels (page 70).

YIELD: 16 Tbsp. Serving Size = 1 Tbsp.

INGREDIENTS

- ½ cup raw cashew halves (120 g)
- ½ cup raw macadamia nuts (70 g)
- 2 Tbsp. organic apple cider vinegar (30 ml)
- 2 Tbsp. fresh lemon juice (30 ml)
- 2-3 Tbsp. water (30 – 45 ml)

Ingredients continued...

DIRECTIONS

1. Place raw nuts in a glass dish. Fill with filtered water. Cover and soak for 24 hours.

2. Drain and rinse.

3. Pour soaked nuts into a blender or food processor. Add vinegar and lemon juice. Blend on low. Add water a little at a time until a smooth mixture is created (about 2 minutes).

4. Set puree aside for one hour.

5. Drape a tall container with two pieces of cheesecloth. The double layer helps create a thicker cream "cheese".

6. Scrape the mixture onto the cheesecloth. Pull up the sides and tie with a piece of string.

7. Hang the tied cheese bag on a wooden spoon and let it drape into a container (ensure it is suspended so the liquids can drain).

8. Leave at room temperature for 24 hours. Then open the cheesecloth and scrape cream "cheese" into a glass container. Store in the fridge.

NUTRITION INFORMATION

72 calories, 6 g fat, 1 g saturated fat, 4 g monounsaturated fat, 1 g polyunsaturated fat, 0 mg cholesterol, 3 g carbohydrate, 2 g NET carbs, 0 g sugar alcohols, 1 g sugar, 1 g fiber, 2 g protein, 67 mg potassium, 53 mg phosphorous, 1 mg sodium, 27 mg magnesium

MACRONUTRIENT RATIO

79% FAT ■ 9% PROTEIN ■ 12% CARBOHYDRATE